CLAIMING THE PAST, SHAPING THE FUTURE

Four Eras in
Liberal Religious Education
1790-1999

Edited by

Roberta M. Nelson

Published by the Liberal Religious Educators Association
in Celebration of its 50th Anniversary

Published by the Liberal Religious Educators Association and
Blackstone Editions, Providence, Rhode Island, 02906
© 2006 by the Liberal Religious Educators Association
All rights reserved. Published 2006
Printed in the United States of America

ISBN: 0-9725017-7-0

This project is funded in part by
the Fund for Unitarian Universalism,
the St. Lawrence Foundation,
the Unitarian Universalist Historical Society,
and the Unitarian Sunday School Society.

CONTENTS

NOTES ON CONTRIBUTORS

M. Elizabeth Anastos. Born in Cambridge, Massachusetts, Elizabeth Anastos graduated from Belmont High School and went on to attend Radcliffe College. Unable to complete her bachelor's degree at that time, she returned to school in the 1980s, graduating in 1987 with a BA from Goddard College in Vermont. In 1973, she was awarded the Angus MacLean Award for excellence in religious education and in 1990 she was awarded an honorary doctorate by Meadville/Lombard Theological School in Chicago, in recognition of more than three decades of commitment to religious education and her many contributions to the work of the Unitarian Universalist Association.

Elizabeth served as Director of Religious Education in three churches, beginning her career in 1959 at Haverill, Massachusetts, and continuing in Weston, Massachusetts from 1962 to 1969. In 1980, while serving at Cedar Lane Unitarian Church in Bethesda, Maryland, she was ordained to the Ministry of Religious Education. Leaving Cedar Lane after eleven years, she continued her service to the Unitarian Universalist Association as Interim Director of the Religious Education Department. For ten years she was Director of Curriculum Development at the UUA, facilitating the creation of new curricula. After retirement she returned to 25 Beacon Street to assume the position of Interim Director of Ministerial Settlement. Her many other contributions to Unitarian Universalist religious education include the presidency of LREDA (Liberal Religious Educators Association), her work with the RE Futures Committee, and her role in the revision of *About Your Sexuality*, the UUA's groundbreaking program in human sexuality.

Hugo J. Hollerorth. The Rev. Dr. Hugo Hollerorth received a BD and MA from the Federated Theological Schools of the University of Chicago in 1949 and 1965, respectively, an EdD from New York University in 1985, and an honorary DD from Meadville/Lombard Theological School in 2005.

After serving as Minister of Education in several United Church of Christ churches during the 1950s, Hollerorth affiliated with the Unitarian Universalist Association. He was the Minister of Education of the Central Unitarian Church of Paramus, New Jersey, from 1959 to 1961; Associate Professor of Religious Education at the St. Lawrence University Theological School from 1961 to 1965; and Director of Curriculum Development in the Division of Education at the UUA from 1965 to 1980.

After joining the UUA staff in 1965, Hollerorth facilitated the development of a religious education curriculum that provided children, youth and adults with "opportunities to orient themselves to the boundlessness and complexity of the power-filled world." His work also ushered in a new direction in religious education curriculum design, known informally as the multimedia kit era. Designed to provide teachers and leaders with a wide variety of materials, strategies, and activities for diverse learning styles and needs, the kits were based on the "discovery method" in educational theory, and covered such complex and critical subjects as decision making, culture building, human heritage, freedom and responsibility, communication, listening, and meaning making. In cooperation with his wife, Dr. Barbara Hollerorth, *The Haunting House* was created. This profoundly religious curriculum invited children and their leaders to explore homes and houses as places of solitude, dreaming, and meaning making.

In the late 1960s, Hollerorth facilitated the development of a sexuality education curriculum for junior high youth. *About*

Your Sexuality pioneered a new era in sexuality education, based on "the best knowledge available of the place of sexuality in the lives of human beings." It used ongoing dialogue and mutual exploration in a process designed for acquiring accurate information, developing communication skills, building attitudes and values, and making responsible decisions in all aspects of sexuality. It supported the worth and dignity of every person and justice for those of differing sexual orientations including gays and lesbians.

Jeanne H. Nieuwejaar. Jeanne Nieuwejaar is a Unitarian Universalist minister of religious education. She was raised in a small Universalist church in rural New England and has remained active in the liberal religious faith throughout her life as lay worker, religious educator and minister. She received her BA in 1966 from Tufts University and her certificate in religious education from the UUA Independent Study Program in 1987. She was fellowshipped and ordained in 1987. From 1987 to 2000, she co-ministered with her husband Olav at the UU congregation in Milford, New Hampshire. She and Olav have also served as interim ministers in Manhasset, New York and Cambridge, England. They are currently directors of the New Hampshire Vermont District of the UUA. They have two sons. Jeanne is the author of *The Gift of Faith: Tending to the Spiritual Needs of Children* (Boston: Skinner House Books, 1999) and, with Marcia Bowen and Richard Stower, of *Life Tapestry* (Boston: UUA, 1994.)

Frank E. Robertson. The reverend Frank Edson Robertson received a BS in Chemical Engineering from Lowell Technical College in 1959, and both his Certificate in Religious Education and his MDiv in Ministry from the Theological School of St. Lawrence University in 1962. He also did graduate studies in world religions at Columbia University and Union Theological Seminary. He was ordained by the Grace Universalist Church in Lowell, Massachusetts in 1962. He has served churches in Barneveld, New York; Shelter Rock, New York; Paramus, New Jersey; Washington, D.C.; Santa Barbara, California; and Evanston, Illinois. In 1998, he retired and was named Minister Emeritus of Religious Education by the Unitarian Church of Evanston.

Frank has served on both the LREDA Board and the UUA board and is a founding member of the Unitarian Universalist History Group. He is a co-author of the curriculum *World Religions*, published by the UUA in 1987.

In 1988 Frank received the IARF award for advancing the work of the Association. In 1998 he received the Angus H. MacLean award for excellence in religious education and the Mark DeWolfe Award for his commitment and exemplary contributions to improving and honoring the lives of bisexual, gay, lesbian, and transgender people.

FOREWORD

The Liberal Religious Educators Association celebrated its fiftieth anniversary at its annual meeting in Plymouth, Massachusetts, October 15-18, 1999. The theme of the conference, "Claiming the Past, Shaping the Future," is truly the theme of this book.

The LREDA 50th Anniversary planning committee invited Jeanne Nieuwejaar, Frank Robertson, Hugo Hollerorth, and Elizabeth Anastos to write papers for presentation at the conference, each representing an era in liberal religious education. The presentation of these papers was a significant part of the program. The committee is deeply grateful to the authors for their understanding of the project and their dedication to documenting the course of religious education and its history. Their papers tell the story of liberal religious education from the latter years of the eighteenth century through the end of the twentieth century.

The papers were prepared for presentation, not publication. Editing them for publication without losing the voices and feelings of the writers has been a balancing act — we hope we have succeeded. With the exception of Elizabeth Anastos, who died in 2004, it has been possible to consult with the authors as we documented material and edited their work. We are grateful for the authors' commitment to the project and their invaluable assistance in bringing this book to completion.

We would like to thank the Fund for Unitarian Universalism, the St. Lawrence Foundation, the Unitarian Universalist Historical Society, and the Unitarian Sunday School Society for the generosity that has made publication of these papers possible.

As editor, I would like to acknowledge the encouragement I have received from my colleagues as I have worked on this project.

I wish to acknowledge with special thanks the generous contributions of Mary Benard, Judith Frediani, Eva Gemmell, Neil Gerdes, Richard Gilbert, Lynn Gordon Hughes, Peter Hughes, John Hurley, Betty Jo Middleton, Eugene Navias, Elizabeth B. Stevens, and Beth Williams.

Finally I extend my deep appreciation to my husband, Christopher, for his patience, determination, encouragement, technical assistance, and editing skills. Without him the project might not have been completed.

Rev. Roberta M. Nelson
Chair, LREDA 50th Anniversary Committee

Jeanne H. Nieuwejaar

❦

THE EARLY YEARS
1790-1930

It is my charge to present to you a history of liberal religious education from its inception up to the beginning of the Fahs/MacLean era. I did hesitate when Roberta Nelson asked me to accept this mission; it seemed a daunting task. I hesitated because I am neither a historian nor a scholar; I am, however, a lover of liberal religious education and I cherish our rootedness in a rich tradition. I honor all those who carved the paths that have led us to this rich, fertile place, where our religious education work can encompass creativity, sexuality, peace and justice, passion and prayer.

This is not, it cannot be, a thorough analysis of the philosophical, methodological, institutional dimensions of religious education through these 140 years. That would be an entire conference, an entire book, and more. Instead I merely survey, opening windows on our early history of religious education. And I visualize this as a process of opening windows on three different levels: first on the foundational level of philosophy, glimpsing the assumptions and ideals that underlay the thinking about religious education; then on the level of curriculum materials and other resources, the tools to implement that philosophy; and finally on the level of lived experience as it is revealed in some wonderful vignettes and remembrances. There is a remarkable incongruence among these three levels—as perhaps there is at every phase of history.

1

There is no clear moment in time when we can claim that our RE history began. There were projects and programs in England in the mid-eighteenth century, but I will bypass those and begin my survey with liberal religion in North America. The work of Benjamin Rush in Philadelphia might be an apt place to claim our beginnings.

Benjamin Rush was a fascinating man who held a place in several religious movements simultaneously and seemingly did so with sincerity and integrity. A significant part of his religious life was with the Universalists, but he worshipped and worked with the Quakers, the Methodists, and the Episcopalians as well. In 1790 in Philadelphia, Rush and a circle of learned and respected men founded a nonsectarian First Day School, or Sunday school. Lisa Friedman says in an unpublished paper, "As these zealous, middle-class Protestants looked at their rapidly changing society, with its increasing population (mostly Catholic immigrants, who, they thought, drank too much) and lack of moral cohesion, they decided that something must be done. Their conclusion was that they were the ones with the time, resources, and moral conviction to do it."[1]

And so, among other things, they established a school to welcome the throngs of children who remained untutored in basic educational matters as well as matters of religion, children who worked all week and simply idled in the streets on Sundays. This was a charitable, ecumenical school, not designed for religious education per se, but religious books were a primary tool there, as in all the schools of that era. Children learned to read from scriptural passages and other religious texts. (In that same year, 1790, the Philadelphia Convention of Universalists supported Rush's resolution endorsing schools for the religious instruction of children.)

The First Day School was an enormous success and was followed by the establishment of several others like it, designed to promote literacy and public virtue through education. Soon there were three in Philadelphia alone, and from there they spread to New York, Rhode Island, Massachusetts, New Hampshire,

Maine, and Delaware. Many of these schools operated out of churches or were run by church men and women. They were not Sunday schools for the training of children in the ways of a particular faith, but they did pave the path.

In 1810 the first known Sunday school established solely for moral and religious instruction was opened in Beverly, Massachusetts, connected with the parish of Rev. Abiel Abbot. It was a Liberal Christian Society — emerging as a Unitarian church. In this school the Bible was the only book of instruction. From this point on, church-based Sunday schools sprang up across the Northeast. Although these schools emerged in all denominations, the Universalist and liberal Christian, later to be known as *Unitarian*, churches led the way even then.

It is no accident that it was the early nineteenth century that saw the proliferation of Sunday schools, as this also was the era when issues around the separation of church and state began to manifest themselves. Public education now began to be defined as secular education, and religious materials could no longer be used casually in public schools (as we well know, the delineation of just what constitutes inappropriately religious materials is a continuing conversation nearly two centuries later). But the doctrinal differences that were emerging, particularly between the Congregationalists and the Unitarians in New England, were making public religious education problematic, and for the first time religious education became the sole responsibility of the church and the family.

The beginnings of the Sunday school movement in this country in the early decades of the nineteenth century coincided with the beginnings of our two denominations as self-conscious religious identities — shortly after the founding of Universalism in America by John Murray in 1770 and shortly before the emergence of American Unitarianism as a separate theological entity and institution.

As these religious schools proliferated, the First Day schools began to disappear, and although the new Sunday Schools were formed for distinctive sectarian purposes, their services were often made available to all the children of the community, reaching out in ways similar to the earlier literacy-oriented schools. The first such Sunday schools were patterned after traditional secular models of education of the time, using memorization and other catechetical techniques, applying these to the learning of Biblical messages.

The new movement in education was not without its critics. Some, such as Samuel Herrick, thought that a school on Sunday "was an infringement on the sanctity of the Sabbath. It was an entering wedge. It required the performance of labor which would soon obliterate all distinction between common and holy time."[2] Others considered it to be an encroachment on the natural territory of the home and the church. In its early days, some considered the Sunday school to be valuable for the poor and criminals but certainly not necessary for the children of respectable families.

So, in the beginning, there was an ambivalent understanding of whom religious education was intended for. This ambivalence was related to questions about who the agents of religious education ought to be. In its 1835 annual report, the Sunday School Society stated "If a Sunday school is to be made a pretense for parents and guardians to neglect the religious education of the children under their care, better would it be that all the Sunday schools should be closed, for they would be stumbling blocks, which would lead many to fall, and prevent the performance of their duty." But this concern was followed by the reassurance that "the religious instruction which children receive in Sunday schools is the cause of more, rather than less attention to the subject on the part of parents, as it awakens in both parents and children an interest which in many instances would otherwise never be roused."[3]

Lewis G. Pray, a Unitarian layman and devoted Sunday school worker, wrote a comprehensive history of the Sunday School in 1847. He describes a room in a Boston Sunday school established "in connection with the ministry of Dr. Tuckerman to the poor" in 1826, during that transitional era when the Sunday Schools had become clearly sectarian but still welcomed many children from the larger community. "The room is fifty feet by forty, furnished with semicircular seats, with maps of Palestine on rollers, and other conveniences, in the most approved style." In this and other rooms, the school comprised, "on an average, at least two hundred and fifty pupils; and the number of its teachers is not usually less than fifty."[4]

The evolution continued, and before too long the Sunday schools tended to be smaller and more clearly identified with the faith of a particular church. At this point, the typical setting might have looked more like this description from the First Church in Roxbury, Massachusetts:

> In the first half of the century the session was only between April first and December first, on account of the lack of heat and the difficulty of sending children any distance in cold and stormy weather. The time of service was sometimes between three and four in the afternoon, but more often before church service in the morning.
>
> The school assembled in the pews in the middle aisle of the church, and the opening exercises generally consisted of a short service with singing. The classes then adjourned to the square pews, where the class lessons were held. Just before the end of the hour they reassembled in the middle aisle, and after repeating the Lord's Prayer and singing a hymn, the school was dismissed with a benediction.[5]

Another image comes from the history of the Unitarian Universalist Church in Buffalo, New York, in which we read that the minister, Dr. Hosmer, "upon the summer evenings ... would have the young people come to his house, and as they were seated about the spacious parlors, or on the floor at his feet, would tell them stories from the Scriptures, or explain some sacred picture on the wall."[6]

By 1827 there were ten Sunday schools in the Unitarian churches of the Boston area, and in that year the Boston Sunday School Society, a gathering of Unitarian ministers and teachers for mutual support and enlightenment and the publishing of books, was formed. The institutionalization of religious education, particularly sectarian religious education, had taken another step forward. As other churches joined this group, *Boston* was dropped from the name. (The organization continues today as the Unitarian Sunday School Society.)

Sunday schools were now firmly established, and the production of appropriate study materials began to take priority. Then as now, the curriculum was but a slice of what constituted the religious nurture of children and youth. However, because it is captured in print, we can know curriculum in a way that we cannot know the tenor of the discussions, the impact of the rituals, or the personal dynamic between child and adult. And because, in many instances, curriculum was sanctioned by some denominational body, it carries an institutional authority and therefore seems the surest route to understanding our religious education history.

But in the matter of curriculum, it is the catechism we must look at first, a form of instruction that predated the Sunday school movement and continued through the nineteenth century — and even into the twentieth. It is a form designed to promote the memorization of doctrine, a form that implicitly affirms that there is a known and provable body of truth, rather than encouraging the student to think for him- or herself. Although its methodology is a clear violation of the liberal religious way, nevertheless catechism was a primary source of religious instruction in our churches for several generations. Catechisms were written by both Unitarians and Universalists, and in later years, when they fell into disfavor as teaching tools, curricula that purported to use a more enlightened method still fell into the mode of rote questions and answers, memorization of factual information, and the articulation of the theology of others. It was clear, however, that other methods and other kinds of resources were needed, and both Unitarians and Universalists began the work of developing more distinctive curricula.

For Universalists, the goal was to teach the clear, hopeful message of their faith in opposition to the evangelical messages of the orthodox. Their catechisms and other works lifted up and extended in particular those passages that paint a picture of a loving, forgiving God.

In 1837 the Universalists of the Boston area formed the Sabbath School Association, but it was not as long-lived and far-reaching as the Unitarian Sunday School Society. State associations helped to strengthen the Sunday school work, but no one central body or authority oversaw the work of curriculum development for the Universalists. This lack of a central body did not deter the publication of materials, however, as both ministers and laymen began to produce texts very early in the century and continued at a steady rate.

In 1830, for instance, Charles Hudson published *Questions on Select Portions of Scripture*, offering extensive Bible quotations followed by two kinds of questions. The first merely ask for a restatement of the meaning of the verse; the second are more interpretive, drawing out theological nuances. The author states that he "has endeavored to make these questions somewhat inductive, but at the same time leaving them in such a manner as to exercise the judgment of the learner."[7] This text was so popular that it was reprinted several times, with printings as late as 1848.

Through most of the nineteenth century, there was agreement within the Universalist movement that the primary subject matter for religious education was the Bible. At first the Bible simply took the place of the catechism as a source of memorization, but soon there appeared question-and-answer lessons applied to the geographical, historical, and social context of the stories, as well as some theological interpretation of Biblical passages. This led to study of the nature of God, Jesus, salvation, etc., and to a concern with the specific moral virtues that are found within the teachings of the Bible.

Although not explicitly claimed as such, references to the natural world as a source of religious truth appear again and again around this time. In his *Questions on Select Portions of Scripture* Hudson says, "The resurrection is a miracle, and so must be above the common course of nature, but is it any more incomprehensible in itself, than the germination of a blade of grass?"[8] Also implicit in these materials is the assumption that humans have the capacity to understand God and his design and to discern their place in this plan. This is a central affirmation of the Universalist faith, and although it is not as clear in the methodology of these early curricula as we might wish, it is there in the underpinnings nevertheless.

On the Unitarian side of our tradition, matters were more centralized and organized. The Sunday School Society began to publish materials in 1828, funded by the American Unitarian Association, which was only three years old. The fact that this fledgling organization made a commitment to religious education is an indication of the importance the Sunday schools had so quickly attained. However, the publishing connection with the AUA was abandoned only three years later, in 1831, as it was found that the name *Unitarian* on the imprint of a book hindered its sales. Thus we find a great range of books published under the more neutral name *Boston Sunday School Society*.

Like those of the Universalists, most of these materials were Biblically based and many were framed in rigid question/ answer patterns. This early curriculum series, which was a little different in tone from the Universalist texts, included Henry Ware Jr.'s *The Life of the Saviour* (1833), which was reprinted at least eight times and widely used more than fifty years later. This narrative tells the life of Jesus in comprehensive detail, following the gospel accounts but with a lot of attention to the social context and literary matters. It is written in an easy, almost chatty, style and heavily laced with the author's interpretations and teachings. For example, "Having dismissed the leper, Jesus left the multitude, and retired to a desert place and prayed. His object probably was both to avoid the throngs of people and give them an opportunity to disperse, and to gain for himself strength and enjoyment from the exercises of devotion. His example teaches us true wisdom—to retire at times from the excitement of the world, and seek light and truth in communion with our hearts and with God."[9]

In 1852 the Sunday School Society published a series of graded lesson manuals with attention to the differing developmental levels of children and youth. This was a pioneering concept, as most materials up to that time did not distinguish between the abilities of the very young and the more mature.

Our look at the religious education materials of the nineteenth century would be incomplete, however, if we were to stop with a consideration of the published curricula. Beginning in the 1820s and continuing throughout the century, there was a prolific flow of periodicals directed to both teachers and parents. As early as 1828, the Unitarians were publishing a monthly titled *The Christian Teacher's Manual*, which was replaced two years later by *The Scriptural Interpreter*. The Universalists published *The Light of Zion and Sabbath School Contributor, The Myrtle, The Sunday School Helper*, and many others. These were filled with philosophical and methodological reflections, advice to teachers, teaching tips, and mountains of materials to be used with the children — hymns, catechisms, nature lessons, and stories — both scriptural and moralistic. A sampling of story titles will suggest the kinds of themes treated: "A Good Girl's Last Days," "The Way to Cure a Fault," "Courage," "The Golden Rule," and "Honor Thy Father and Thy Mother."

Several purposes were stated for religious education in these years, but most often we find that the work was aimed at character formation. A writer in *The Sunday School Teacher and Children's Friend* says, "Let the teacher remember that his ultimate object is not the communication of knowledge, but the formation of character — that he is to have reference not so much to the intellect as to the heart."

If character formation was the goal, the means toward that goal was not only the curriculum but also modeling. Children were offered stories and biographies to follow, but the behavior of the teachers themselves was also understood to be a significant influence: "The silent influence of a correct manner in the teachers will be seen in the deportment of the children."[10]

It is interesting to note that, although the direct aim of the Sunday schools was toward the education of the children, in fact they had a broad influence, affecting parents and teachers as well: "All who are concerned in teaching Sunday school pupils receive more or less instruction from it themselves, especially the teachers, who perhaps derive more benefit from it than those taught. Parents also come in for their share, because they are called upon to aid their children in their preparation for the school, and some parents, I doubt not, thus receive more useful religious instruction than in any other way."[11]

The images of teacher training that emerge from the histories of nineteenth-century churches suggest that often this was a wonderfully strong piece of the religious education movement. It was not unusual for teachers to gather weekly, often with the minister, for scriptural study and for their own personal growth and education. There were area groupings as well for training and support. Our forebears realized early on that the text alone was but a slight piece of the educational process.

The position of Sunday school teacher was an esteemed one. In his discourse "The Sunday-School," William Ellery Channing wrote, "Like all schools, the Sunday-school must owe its influence to its teachers ... the most gifted in our congregation cannot find a worthier field of labor than the Sunday-school."[12]

A new understanding of the young mind and soul was emerging in the nineteenth century, even as the Sunday school became more established. The flourishing of Transcendentalism—that piece of our history peopled by Ralph Waldo Emerson, Henry Thoreau, Bronson Alcott, Theodore Parker, Lydia Maria Child, Elizabeth Palmer Peabody, and William Ellery Channing—was a joyous and energizing burst in the liberal religious movement. It was a religious philosophy that affirmed an unabashed celebration of childhood. The naturalness, freshness, and simplicity of a child's perceptions of and responses to the world suggested to the Transcendentalists that childhood was a time of purer divinity, clearer and more honest contact with the power of holiness within them, ultimate wisdom, and a kind of spiritual knowing that would become cluttered and confused and faded as children grew older.

The notion that the soul of the infant comes into this world from a direct experience of existing with God, knowing God in a more total way than is possible in this earthly life, was central to Transcendental thought. In this view, the work of religious education was largely that of eliciting what was already within the child, an innate knowledge of God and of goodness.

William Ellery Channing's well-known 1837 statement on "The Sunday-School" is a beautiful and enduring articulation of this philosophy: "The great end in religious instruction … is not to stamp *our* minds irresistibly on the young, but to stir up their own … All the elementary ideas of God and duty and love and happiness come to [the child] from his own spiritual powers and affections. Moral good and evil, virtue and vice, are revealed to him in his own motives of action and in the motives of those around him."[13]

Even prior to Channing's address we find this theme articulated in the literature, as in this passage from the *Christian Teacher's Manual* of 1828. The teacher is "not to infuse a soul into the little being before him, but to bring out the soul that is there in its native purity, and exercise it, and make himself acquainted with it … A most important qualification [for teachers] is … a deep reverence for the minds of children … the soul is there in all its beauty and perfection, waiting only for time and opportunity to put forth all its strength." In the same year we find another religious educator saying, "Our object is to awaken and call forth the mind to action, and give it such impressions of virtue and holiness as shall advance its progress … the course to obtain this, is to lead the minds of the young to think for themselves, rather than overburthen them with the thoughts of others."[14]

The role of religious education and of the Sunday school teacher, then, was to support and nurture the child in his or her own religious unfolding, using primarily the wisdom and truth of scripture and the modeling of the teacher's own life, and engaging the child in active and experiential dialogue. Although these ideals may not have been lived out in any broad way in the Sunday schools of the liberal Christian churches, they did offer a clear philosophy far removed from that which underlay the catechetical method sanctioned for use in the orthodox churches.

Lofty sentiments were proclaimed, as in Channing's historic address. The realities in the local churches were that the path was ragged, with some churches maintaining a kind of energy and rigor that eluded others. Although curriculum is the usual way to teach the philosophy of a religious tradition, this thinking is reflected more clearly in other dimensions of the religious education experience in both Universalist and Unitarian histories.

Rituals celebrating childhood are an important piece of our heritage. Child dedications date from very early years, at least in the Universalist tradition. John Murray wrote that "Children were God's children" and designed a public ceremony to recognize that fact.[15] Although the dedication services in early service books were often heavy and oppressive, the spirit that prompted them was an affirming and celebratory one.

Children's Day, that great and lasting tradition, was established in 1857 by Rev. Charles H. Leonard of the Universalist Church in Chelsea, Massachusetts. Twelve years later, the delegates to the Universalist General Convention, by formal vote, set apart the second Sunday in June as a day to be marked regularly as Children's Day. Also known as Flower Sunday, Rose Sunday, Lily Sunday, and other titles, this was a time to honor the children's presence and participation in the church community.

Libraries were a significant part of the early Sunday schools. Fund-raising efforts were devoted to building library collections and committees were formed for screening and selecting books. It was not until late in the nineteenth century that public libraries became widespread, so the Sunday school collections were real community treasures. Intended primarily as resources for the people of the church, they extended beyond that circle as well. In the Unitarian movement, a Ladies Commission on Sunday School Books was formed in 1868 to prepare a catalogue of books approved for Sunday schools and libraries. From that time, at least through the turn of the century, the Commission published annual lists of approved books. In thirty-four years 10,957 books were examined, of which 3,076 were approved.[16]

Charitable work is another strong thread in this fabric of Sunday school life. In our time, social action is often remote from those who receive the benefits, but in earlier times, this was a neighborhood matter. Consciousness of poor children and families and active outreach to them was pervasive, sometimes in the form of collections and gifts of food or clothing, but also often in the form of reaching out to include the poor in the life of the church and its educational and social programs. This was seen not as evangelizing work but as a sharing of good fortune.

In a history of the First Unitarian Church of Baltimore, we read of the establishment of the Children's Christian Union in 1881, an extension of the Sunday School. This organization was founded out of concern that there were "a number of children connected with our Sunday School whose homes are poor, and whose advantages are limited." The following quote is worth sharing:

> Meetings of the Union were held once a month in the evening. Children eleven years of age or older were invited with their parents and older sisters ... Activities consisted of a formal program with music, a lecture, ... readings, recitations and refreshments. The formal program concluded, every available room in the Chapel was occupied with stereotypical viewing, illustrated books and magazines, quiet games, story telling, instruction in fancy work and carpentry. Gardening was encouraged by the distribution of seeds and bulbs, and a lecture on planting. Books were available from a circulating library of four hundred and fifty volumes. Attendance often ran as high as one hundred and twenty.

The minutes of the Union noted

> the benefit of these meetings, not only to the children, but also to those poor hardworking mothers, to whom books and pictures are costly curiosities, to whom a good cup of coffee is a rare event, and to whom an evening spent in a larger place, welcomed into it by kindly words and faces, lifted for a while above the dead dry level of their daily lives, a blessing of which we have no conception.[17]

Likewise, the Sunday school movement had a lively social component, with many churches organizing picnics, parties, and annual excursions by boat or train to some site where lunches were served and games and sports, as well as religious exercises, singing, and addresses, were organized. In the history of the Universalist church of Buffalo, New York, we read of a summer excursion in 1843 that was organized as a fund-raiser for the Sunday School. The trip to Fort Schlosser was planned by a committee of fifty ladies and gentlemen, and more than 1,500 attendees were reported. "Five clergymen from three denominations, Universalists, Unitarians, and Christians were present," and about $200 was raised to purchase books for the school.[18] Of course, there were more intimate parties, dances, picnics, and outings as well, and it was common for courtships to develop in these settings.

The energy and clarity of the Sunday School movement, at least in the Northeast, waned somewhat from the 1860s through the 1880s, in part perhaps because the Civil War era drained both money and energy. In 1888 the Universalists established a Sunday School Commission to review the condition of their religious education programs and to make recommendations to the General Convention. The Commission's report in 1889 acknowledges an unresolved struggle "as to aims and methods." And it continues, "It is by no means a clear and simple problem to decide what we are to do with the machinery which has been created within a century, a machinery potent for the most signal results if rightly used, capable of incalculable waste if ill-adjusted or blindly operated." The Commission found two divergent theories of religious instruction, the imparting of instruction and the exercising of moral influence, but found that these two goals need not be in conflict but could be mutually supportive. They remained clearly committed to use of the Bible as the appropriate source of truth, with the child led to model his or her own life after the noble values upheld in its stories.[19]

The International Uniform Lessons, a nondenominational curriculum, was widely used from 1872 in both Unitarian and

Universalist churches. These scripture-based lessons were designed to standardize the religious education program, coordinating a seven-year cycle in which all Sunday school children, regardless of denominational affiliation, studied the same Biblical passage each week. It was a massive interdenominational effort that was successful on many levels. The Universalists created their own guide to this curriculum.[20]

But a desire for more liberal lessons continued and, based on the recommendations of a 1901 commission, a strong staff of ministers and lay persons created the Universalist Graded Lessons. These were primarily but not exclusively focused on the Bible. They were followed in 1908 by the Murray Graded Lessons, which offered a still more modern series.[21]

The Unitarians continued to publish curricula, and although it is supposed that the rigidities of catechism had long ago been abandoned, in fact some of the materials of this era continue that tradition. For instance, James Freeman Clarke's 1884 *Manual of Unitarian Belief* offers discussion questions that merely ask for a parroting back of information, although it claims that it is intended to prompt discussion.

In 1883, however, we find Charles C. Everett's *Religions Before Christianity*, which introduces the student to Buddhism, Hinduism, Islam, and other faiths. These faiths are reflected largely in the light of Christianity, but this is a significant step toward honoring the other religions of the world. And in a very different mode, in 1884 Charles Dole published *The Citizen and the Neighbor*, based on the idea that "the spirit and ethical principles of religion ought to be made to apply especially to the solution of social and political questions."[22]

Biographies became increasingly popular teaching tools during the nineteenth century, as a way to present truths through personal narrative. They had always been important in the libraries and surfaced from time to time in the curricula as well. In his 1892 work *Noble Lives and Noble Deeds*, Edward A. Horton notes that "religion rests at last on the individual."[23] Each biography in this collection lifts up some moral trait and is followed by discussion questions. Most of these questions are merely factual, but a few open possibilities for a more reflective kind of conversation.

Edward A. Horton, president of the Sunday School Society in 1892, urged churches to adopt more progressive methods of education and to abandon catechisms and base their work on a greater trust in the child and to aim at developing reliance on an inner rather than an outer authority.[24] He urged churches to value the child's natural sense of wonder and curiosity, but we find little of his philosophy reflected in the curricula or periodical literature of that era. The Bible was regarded as the source of truth, accompanied by set statements of Unitarian belief, and rote learning was the method of instruction. The ideals of the Transcendentalists, the faith in the pure soul of the child, had all but disappeared from the work of religious education.

But other liberalizing influences were felt. One of these was the Western movement in both Unitarianism and Universalism, which was less rooted in traditional assumptions and moved more easily beyond the notion that religion should concern itself only with Christianity. This movement was open to seeing all of life, in the human and the natural world, as religious.

In the 1870s, the Western movement was influential in originating and spreading Unity Clubs for young adults. These groups were formed for both literary and religious study, as well as for social activities. From there it was a short step to the Young People's Religious Union, an early precursor of today's Young Religious Unitarian Universalists.

Beyond our denomination, other influences were beginning to manifest themselves as well, influences that would strengthen Horton's voice and begin to challenge and transform thinking about religious education. After the turn of the century a shift in religious consciousness began, and this shift was reflected in the Sunday schools.

This was a time of intellectual ferment both in our own country and abroad, an era of progressive, scientific orderliness following the publication of Charles Darwin's theories. John

Dewey's educational theories undermined the status of content in our religious education, giving way to a new understanding of process—although this had surely been foreshadowed by Channing—and to greater attention to children's interests and developmental levels. The 1893 World Congress of Religion in Chicago was a major breakthrough in interfaith dialogue, which began to be reflected in curriculum. And the work of Biblical scholarship opened doors, allowing deeper understandings of the Bible as a human construct.

So in 1909, although there were then 125 books actively in use in Unitarian Sunday schools, religious educators felt a growing need for a new series, one that would honor some of the new values and provide a logical progression throughout the developmental years. Thus the first Beacon Series in religious education was published, with courses for each grade from 1 to 12. In this series we find a much more sensitive kind of attention paid to graded lessons, the beginnings of handwork for young children—although it amounted to little more than pages to be colored—and Biblical study informed by the scholarship of the era.

Now the study of Jesus was framed as "Jesus of Nazareth" rather than "The Life of Our Savior."[25] Joel H. Metcalf's *World Stories*, a sort of precursor to Sophia Fahs's *From Long Ago and Many Lands*, further opened the door to an appreciation of religious wisdom beyond the Biblical, Christian focus that had prevailed up to that time; and *Comparative Studies in Religion: An Introduction to Unitarianism* by Henry T. Secrist broadened the understanding of other faiths, although with reference to Christianity as the center of concern.

In 1913 the Universalists' General Sunday School Association was established as the first centrally based organization in the denomination for overseeing and promoting religious education efforts. In an era of radical change in pedagogical theories, the Association was a steady force for the transition from a Bible-centered to a child-centered approach, with a new appreciation of experiential methods.

In 1912 the AUA established a Department of Education, which took over from the Unitarian Sunday School Society the primary responsibility for publishing curricula. The counsel of Edwin Starbuck, a revolutionary thinker in the work of psychology and education, was solicited, and soon yet another curriculum series was launched — the New Beacon Course. In this series we see a marked evolution in the presentation of material. Teachers' guides accompanied some of the books, and goals, necessary materials, and other helpful hints were clearly articulated for each lesson, at least in the volumes for young children.

The emphasis in religious education is now less on Biblical material and more on character formation. There is a greater interest in the child's own experience and a real concern for the contemporary world and its problems. One book for young children, *God's Wonder World* by Cora Stanwood Cobb (1918), makes the celebration of nature explicit. We still find a content-centered, largely didactic approach to teaching, but a shift has taken place, and stronger currents are about to be felt. Just as an aside, I would note that I found in *A Friendly World* (1926) a story, author unknown, titled "Bringing the Milk to the Babies," in which a little engine plowed through a great snowstorm and up a great hill, puffing, "I think I can, I think I can."[26]

To round out this glimpse of our earliest history, it is instructive to look at passages from historic religious education materials that show how many of the woes we encounter plagued our forebears as well. One of the Boston Sunday Schools noted in 1829, "Teachers can do but little in the short time allowed them, without the cordial cooperation of the parents and guardians at home."[27] In an 1849 survey of the Sunday School Society, one respondent wrote, "It is difficult to procure good teachers, and it is about as difficult to assign a good reason for it. We should bear in mind that 'labors of love' in every community are usually performed by a few and these few are generally not persons of wealth or leisure." Other responses included: "Good teachers become disheartened by the lack of parental sympathy and cooperation," "Want of culture in the willing: want of will and piety in the otherwise gifted," and "Who can teach that which he has never learned?" In response to a question on parental involvement: "Some mothers take an interest, but most fathers regard it with indifference."[28] And finally, a report of the Unitarian Society of Albany in the year 1900 states, "Too many stay away when it rains, and then when it is a nice clear day, because it is a nice clear day."[29]

NOTES

[1] Private communication.

[2] Quoted in Joella Vreeland, *This Is the Church: The Story of a Church, a Community, and a Denomination: First Universalist Church, Southold, New York* (Mattituck, NY: Amereon House, 1988), 215.

[3] Unitarian Sunday School Society, *The Seventh Annual Report of the Sunday School Society* (Boston, 1835), 26-27.

[4] Lewis G. Pray, *The History of Sunday Schools and of Religious Education from the Earliest Times* (Boston, 1847), 222.

[5] Walter Eliot Thwing, *History of the First Church in Roxbury, Massachusetts, 1603–1904* (Boston, 1908), 354–355.

[6] Charles P. Jamieson, *Heritage of Heresy: Unitarian Universalist Church of Buffalo, N.Y. 1832-1982* (Kenmore, NY: Partners Press, 1982), 24.

[7] Charles Hudson, *Questions on Select Portions of Scripture*, 2nd ed. (Boston, 1835), v.

[8] Hudson, *Questions on Select Portions of Scripture*, 114.

[9] Henry Ware Jr., *The Life of the Saviour* (Boston, 1833), 96.

[10] *Sunday School Teacher and Children's Friend* 3 (1837), 298-299.

[11] Unitarian Sunday School Society, *Seventh Annual Report*, 27.

[12] William Ellery Channing, "The Sunday-School: Discourse pronounced before the Sunday-School Society" in *Works of William E. Channing, D.D.* (Boston: AUA, 1882), 458.

[13] Channing, "The Sunday-School," 449–450.

[14] Unitarian Sunday School Society, *Second Annual Report of the Boston Sunday School Society* (Boston, 1829), 17.

[15] John Murray, *The Life of Rev. John Murray* (8th edition; Boston, 1851), 151. Murray discusses the child dedication ceremony in *Letters and Sketches of*

Sermons, included in the Addenda to this edition, 319-321. See also Richard Eddy, *Universalism in America* (Boston, 1894), 1:235-237.

[16] George Willis Cooke, *Unitarianism in America* (Boston: AUA, 1902), 281.

[17] Rebecca Funk and the historical committee of the church, *A Heritage to Hold in Fee: First Unitarian Church of Baltimore (Universalist and Unitarian)* (Baltimore: Garamond Press, 1962), 83-84.

[18] Jamieson, *Heritage of Heresy,* 26-27.

[19] Universalist General Convention, *Minutes of the Universalist General Convention: Session of 1889 — Lynn, Mass.,* 65-66. Microfilm 4080, Andover-Harvard Theological Library.

[20] James Minton Pullman, *Studies in the Life and Teachings of Jesus: For Sunday Schools* (Lynn, MA, 1894).

[21] Clinton Lee Scott, *The Universalist Church of America: A Short History* (Boston: Universalist Historical Society, 1957), 48-49.

[22] Charles F. Dole, *The Citizen and the Neighbor* (Boston: Unitarian Sunday School Society, 1884), iii.

[23] Edward A. Horton, *Noble Lives and Noble Deeds* (Boston: Unitarian Sunday School Society, 1893), iii.

[24] Unitarian Sunday School Society, *Annual Report of the Board of Directors for 1893* (Boston, 1894), 3.

[25] Charles Edwards Park, *Jesus of Nazareth* (Boston: Unitarian Sunday School Society, 1909).

[26] "Bringing the Milk to the Babies," in Ethel Franklin and Annie E. Pousland, *A Friendly World* (Boston: Beacon Press, 1926), 96-98.

[27] Unitarian Sunday School Society, *Annual Reports of the Boston Sunday School Society for the Year 1829* (Boston, 1830), 6.

[28] Unitarian Sunday School Society, *Twenty-second Annual Report of the Sunday School Society* (Boston, 1850), 12, 13, 16.

[29] George T. Waterman, *Reports to the Congregation of the First Unitarian Society of Albany,* 1900.

Frank E. Robertson

THE FAHS/MACLEAN ERA 1930-1965

It is a special honor to be among those who are helping to celebrate the fiftieth anniversary of LREDA by presenting introductions to the history of liberal religious education in our movement. Thank you. My focus is on what has been called "the Fahs/MacLean Era," named of course after Sophia Lyon Fahs and Angus Hector MacLean, whose leadership flourished among us from the 1930s through the early 1960s. I was privileged to know them both during my years as a student at St. Lawrence University Theological School. Sophia was a visiting professor briefly in 1961, and Angus was in his final year of service as dean during my first year.

Angus had a long association with St. Lawrence. He was professor of religious education from 1928 to 1951 and then dean until his semi-retirement in 1960, when he went to the First Unitarian Church of Cleveland to work half-time fashioning ways to encourage parents to get to know each other in small groups and to become more intentional about the religious education of their children.[1]

At St. Lawrence Angus had been the central force in developing a full training program for directors of religious education. Most ministerial students took that program as well as general ministerial studies, receiving dual credentials upon graduation — certification in religious education and a graduate degree in ministry, then called the bachelor of divinity degree. Our studies in religious education included courses in the philosophy of education, child growth and development theory, curriculum development, and the use of the creative arts in religious education, as well as two years of supervised field work, usually teaching classes at the local Universalist Church in Canton, New York, or advising the Channing-Murray Group of young adults.[2] Several of us enriched our training by serving on the staff of Camp Unirondack for one or more of the summers during our seminary years. During our senior year, each of us served as minister at one of the small churches in upstate New York on weekends. Generally we were on our own to sink or swim, come what may, with guidance if we asked for it. I marvel at what those churches put up with. Many of us were rather green and inexperienced. The congregations were more our teachers than we were their ministers.

I recall a story about Angus that typified his style: Professor Max Kapp, professor of homiletics at the time, was in Angus's office on a warm autumn day when a big bumblebee flew in the window right at them. Max quickly got up on a chair and began swatting in all directions with a newspaper, as the terrified bee zoomed around them. Eventually, Angus calmly went over to the bee, gently cupped his hands around it, and released it out the window. Angus's living philosophy seems to me to have been an effort to give others gentle encouragement toward freeing themselves to find their own ways in life.

My memory of Sophia Fahs's visit to St. Lawrence is rather limited. I only recall that her visit was considered to be of major importance at the school, and I can picture her somewhat stern presence at the head of the seminar table. I wonder now what she really thought of our training program in religious education. Certainly it was the best opportunity available in its day[3] but it did not measure up to the level of scientific research and curriculum experimentation she envisioned in her proposals to the Unitarian Universalist Association and to various Unitarian Universalist seminaries, during her later years, for a center for the study of religious education.[4] She had very high standards but a cordial dignity that made others wish they could measure up to those standards.

A few years after that initial meeting, I bumped into Sophia one day in the library of Union Theological Seminary in New York City. She was burdened with about a dozen books and shared how excited she was about discovering religious implications in the cave paintings of Neanderthal people. There she was, ninety-something, wide-eyed with enthusiasm for some new learning she had discovered about the ancient origins of religion. She seemed nineteen, not ninety, and I marveled at her vitality. She lived just a few blocks away from where I lived in Morningside Heights, and I was fortunate to share several visits with her during the mid-1960s.

Both Sophia and Angus studied at Teachers College of Columbia University. Sophia obtained her master's degree in education there in 1904 and her bachelor of divinity degree from Union Theological Seminary in 1926.[5] Angus received his doctor of philosophy degree from Columbia's Teachers College in 1930, having graduated from the Theological School of McGill University in 1923.[6] Both had Presbyterian backgrounds and both were indebted to John Dewey as the primary source of their philosophies of religious education. Both were born outside the United States: Sophia was born to missionary parents in China on August 2, 1876,[7] and Angus was born on Cape Breton Island in Nova Scotia, Canada, in 1892.[8] Sophia entered our movement via the Unitarians; Angus entered our movement via the Universalists.

Of Sophia's and Angus's writing on the philosophy of religious education and its application, Sophia's *Today's Children and Yesterday's Heritage* and *Worshipping Together with Questioning Minds* are most familiar to us today. Less well-known but equally brilliant are Angus's *The New Era in Religious Education: A Manual for Church School Teachers* and *The Wind in Both Ears*.

During her long life of 102 years, Sophia published over seventy writings. Her first book, *Uganda's White Man of Work*, in 1907, introduced biography into evangelical Christian literature for children and was extremely popular, used by about forty denominations.[9] Some of Sophia's more popular pamphlets from the 1950s and 1960s were *The Beginnings of Mysticism in Children's Growth, Why Teach Religion in an Age of Science?, A New Ministry to Children,* and *Developing Concepts of God with Children.* One wonders how different our movement might have been if, when they were in Germany in 1912, Sophia's husband Charles had not decided to book tickets back to the United States on the *Rotterdam* because he felt that second-class tickets on the *Titanic* were too expensive![10]

Two important pamphlets written by Angus in the early 1950s were *Planning the Religious Education Curriculum: Some Basic Considerations* and *The Method Is the Message.* Angus's most famous teaching is encapsulated in that second title: *The Method Is the Message.* In the 1962 version of it he wrote,

> The subject matter may be what you please at any time. The Joseph story on the 8-year-old level, *The Drama of Ancient Israel* at a more advanced age, etc., but since our methods communicate the values implicit in them, such matters as love, the ability to reason, the experience and appreciation of freedom, mutual tolerance and understanding, justice, etc., must be taught by being used all the time in all the classes and all the courses. If anything was ever worthy of being called the "core curriculum" this is.[11]

Toward the end of his pamphlet, Angus advises teachers to read each unit of a given curriculum carefully, tag the basic value implied, and find a creative way to experience that value with the children before using the unit or sharing the story as an illustration.

Such advice is very much the application of the progressive education theory of John Dewey to liberal religious education. Angus required that his students read at least Dewey's *The Child and the Curriculum* and urged us to read his other books, such as the great classic *Democracy and Education: An Introduction to the Philosophy of Education.* St. Lawrence graduate Richard Gilbert recalls being in one of Angus's classes on a particularly nice warm day when Angus jumped at the suggestion that they all go bird-watching, one of his favorite pastimes.[12] Students remember such experiences with fondness and, upon later reflection, speak of them as illustrations of his Deweyan philosophy.

At the start of her teaching career, Sophia was influenced by Teachers College faculty who shared John Dewey's philosophy. Many of them were part of the founding of the Religious Education Association in 1903 when Dewey gave an address.[13] In a recent interview with Verna Carncross, former director of religious education of the Universalist-Unitarian Church of Utica, New York, and now in her nineties, she said, "I know why I was so successful using Sophie's [Sophia's] books in our church school. I had read John Dewey and understood how to create a program using his philosophy."[14]

At the beginning of the Fahs/MacLean Era in 1930, there were two professionals working for the Department of Religious Education of the American Unitarian Association: Waitstill Sharp, the department head in Boston, and his associate, Edwin Fairley, who was working out of New York. Waitstill had encouraged the establishment of several summer institutes for the training of teachers, including the first such institute at Star Island in the Isles of Shoals, in 1921. Edwin Fairley was familiar with religious educators in the New York City area, including those associated with Teachers College, and he invited Sophia Fahs to be a leader of the 1930 summer institute at Star Island.[15] That marked the entrance of Sophia into the Unitarian community.

There were two religious education curriculum evaluation committees of the Department of Religious Education in the early 1930s; one met in Boston with Waitstill Sharp and the other met in New York with Edwin Fairley. Sophia is known to have attended some of the meetings of the one in New York but was not a formal member.[16]

Dorothy Tilden Spoerl, a new young light on the religious education horizon, represented the Universalists on the committee in Boston.[17] Dorothy had been director of religious education of the Universalist Church of Detroit before moving to

Boston and obtaining a job from Waitstill working with children in the North End Union, sponsored by the Benevolent Fraternity of Unitarian Churches.[18]

In October of 1931, the two committees met together in Philadelphia and agreed on the following aims and ideas for religious education:

- To *think* clearly on the meaning of human experience as revealed in history, literature, the arts and sciences.
- To *feel* the reality, harmony and nobility of the universe, as revealed in Nature and Personality.
- To *discipline* ourselves for the highest service which we may render.[19]

Such a list of purposes was revolutionary in 1931.

In May of 1933, the Boston committee discovered the dynamic director of religious education of the Congregational Church School of Newtonville, Massachusetts, Ernest W. Kuebler.[20] Ernest would become secretary of the Department of Religious Education of the American Unitarian Association in 1935, which was another way of saying he was head of the department. Meanwhile, the Great Depression had hit the country. Waitstill Sharp and Edwin Fairley were out of work and the two committees disbanded.

The Universalist Church of America was experiencing an upswing in religious education following a decline during the first two decades of the century, even though the adult membership continued to decline. That rise appears to have been due to the work of the General Sunday School Association (GSSA), led by George E. Huntley from 1913 to 1929, and the field work of Harriet G. Yates from 1921 into the 1930s. George Huntley had served on the faculty of St. Lawrence (then called Canton Theological School) while also serving as the first president of the GSSA. He resigned from the faculty in 1917 to devote all of his energies to the Universalist Sunday school movement.[21]

Also at the beginning of the Fahs/MacLean Era, the first formal step was taken toward the joining together of the Unitarian (Young People's Religious Union) and Universalist (Young

People's Christian Union) youth movements. In 1930 a Joint Commission on Social Responsibility was created; it was ratified in 1933.[22] The YPRU and the YPCU appointed co-chairs and equal numbers from each group served on the Commission, even though the Unitarians outnumbered the Universalists four to one in that period. Dana Greeley (later to become president of the AUA and the UUA) and Max Kapp (later to become the last dean of the St. Lawrence University Theological School) were the respective presidents of the two youth groups. Members of both groups joined a peace caravan sponsored by the American Friends Service Committee in 1934.[23]

In the same year, the American Unitarian Association formed a Commission of Appraisal headed by Frederick May Eliot, then minister of Unity Church of St. Paul and later president of the AUA. He was a strong advocate for religious education. The Commission's report of 1936, entitled "Unitarians Face a New Age," called for a greater emphasis on religious education and proposed "that the entire church program shall be redefined in terms of education."[24]

Parallel to the work of the Commission, Ernest Kuebler appointed a new Curriculum Study Committee, which produced a statement of objectives at the same May Meetings in 1936. This statement called for "the development in children and young people of an intelligent faith, strong character, the appreciation of values, church participation, and an improved social order."[25] That statement and the 1931 aims would become the platform for the Fahs/MacLean era.

In February of 1937, with the strong recommendation of the new Curriculum Study Committee, Sophia Fahs was hired half-time as the editor of children's materials for the Department of Religious Education.[26] Initially, Sophia was hired to help Ernest Kuebler and the Committee revise the old Beacon Course, but she soon convinced them that a whole new Beacon series of curricula was needed. She wrote her now-famous *Beginnings of Earth and Sky* as the first book in what would come to be called the New Beacon Series.[27] Published in 1937 by Beacon Press, this book contains creation stories from folklore and world religions, which Sophia had gathered over the years while teaching in the experimental Sunday school of Teachers College, working in the Union Theological Seminary's School of Religion, and serving on the Sunday school staff of the new liberal Protestant Riverside Church (formerly Park Avenue Baptist Church).[28] Toward the end of the book, Sophia added "Sir Isaac Newton's Story" and "A Modern Scientist's Story." To include scientific creation theory with ancient creation stories and to view them both as stages in the human search for the truth was radical for that time.

Sophia continued teaching courses in religious education at Union and serving on the staff of Riverside Church in New York while traveling back and forth to Boston. She retired as supervisor of the Junior Department at Riverside Church in 1942.[29]

In 1937 Sophia came across an article written by Dorothy Spoerl in the Universalist publication, *The Christian Leader*. It reported on a church school course Dorothy had devised on some of the mythological stories in James Frazier's *The Golden Bough*.[30] It was clear to Sophia that she had found a soul mate. She contacted Dorothy and invited her to work with her on the next book for the New Beacon Series, *Beginnings of Life and Death*. Thus began the collaboration of two of our movement's greatest women.

The last chapter, "Our Own Wonderings about Death," includes this touching poem written in 1918 by Sophia's daughter Ruth at the age of eleven:

> Where is the really, really me?
> I'm somewhere, I know, but where can that be?
> I'm not my nose, nor my mouth, nor my eye,
> I'm not my feet, nor my legs, nor my thigh.
> I'm not my hand, nor my arm, nor my hip,
> And I'm not my teeth, nor my tongue, nor my lip.
> I'm sure I'm not my elbow or knee—
> Oh, where am I? Oh, where can I be?[31]

Sadly, Ruth died of infantile paralysis in 1920. Later Sophia would reflect, "Had it not been for this personal tragedy, I would never have had the courage, I believe, to think of putting the word 'death' on the title page of a children's book."[32]

Sophia and one of her teachers from Riverside Church, Mildred T. Tenny, wrote teachers' guides to the two books, and the books became very popular, going through several editions. Eventually they were combined into one volume, *Beginnings: Earth, Sky, Life, Death* (1958) with a separate new teachers' guide entitled *Exploring Beginnings* (1960) by Mildred Tester and Lucile Lindberg, based on the previous guides and on suggestions gathered from over two decades of use by teachers of fourth and fifth graders across the continent.[33]

Two books for teenagers that Sophia did not edit but that continued her world-centered approach were *Primitive Faiths* (1937) and *Hinduism* (1938), by Elizabeth MacDonald. These books were written in an old workbook style. When the committee began to shift over to more extensive separate teachers' guides, they decided not to reprint them after copies ran out.[34]

Frances Wood, who was brought on board as field secretary at the Department of Religious Education in 1937, improved communications about these new materials.[35] Frances had been the director of religious education at the Unitarian Church of Detroit. Dorothy Spoerl had known of her excellent leadership qualities while in Detroit in 1928 and 1929.[36] Frances had also been serving on the AUA's Religious Education Committee since 1935.[37] She would go on to visit numerous churches and area gatherings of Unitarians across the continent, interpreting the New Beacon Series for the next two decades.

Ernest Kuebler and Sophia Fahs sent out an open letter to all ministers and church school workers in 1939, explaining their plans and soliciting potential authors.[38] Their plans included a series of biographies on Moses, Akhenaton, Socrates, Confucius, Gandhi, Jane Addams, Booker T. Washington, Albert Schweitzer, Jesus (one for children under twelve and one for teens), and others, written for older children and youth and accompanied by teachers' guides. Some of these books would never be written. It was difficult to find authors who had the depth of scholarship Sophia demanded but who could also write for young people.

The first of the series, *Child of the Sun* (1939) was on the ancient Egyptian pharaoh, Akhenaton. Again the author was one of Sophia's teachers, Margaret Dulles Edwards, and the story had been used with upper elementary children under Sophia's guidance at Riverside Church.[39]

In 1938 Sophia began a new research project with the nursery and kindergarten staff at Riverside Church. She and the teachers began to create a list of young children's concerns and the experiences that seemed to be most important to the children, "times when the children seemed emotionally wistful, or puzzled, or curious, or eager for larger understanding."[40] She asked for input from a number of authorities in the field, including Abigail Eliot (sister of Frederick May Eliot), director of the Nursery Training School of Boston. Abigail Eliot introduced her to Verna Hills, a graduate of the school, who agreed to write some stories about the children's concerns.[41] Those stories, published in 1939, became the first of the pioneering *Martin and Judy* series.

In the summer of 1938, Sophia met another specialist on young children at the Religious Education Conference at Star Island — Elizabeth Manwell, professor of the psychology of preschool children at Syracuse University and director of religious education at the Unitarian Church of Syracuse. Sophia shared Verna's stories with Elizabeth, and the two began a collaboration that led to their co-authorship of *Consider the Children: How They Grow*, a pioneering book for parents and specialists in the field of early childhood education. The book stands on its own but frequently refers to the stories in the *Martin and Judy* series. Elizabeth Manwell joined the Curriculum Committee of the AUA and served on it for more than twenty years.[42]

Sophia came to write some of the stories herself and co-authored the second and third volumes with Verna Hills. The books were a great success, going through numerous editions, and were used by other denominations and private schools. Dorothy Spoerl, Elizabeth Maxwell, and Margaret Price wrote the first teachers' guides, followed by Josephine Gould in 1951. Indeed, the books were so popular among children that there is evidence that they replaced the usual Bible stories in many homes.[43]

At the first church I served, in Barneveld, New York, one of the church school teachers overheard through an open window the conversation of two four-year-olds playing outside Unity Hall. A neighboring Catholic girl was playing with one of the Unitarian boys. She asked him, "What do you learn in your Sunday school? We learn about Mary and Joseph." The Unitarian boy answered with deep sincerity, "Oh, we learn about the same thing, only we call them Martin and Judy."

Responding somewhat to criticism that the series should include more traditional content, the authors included the stories "Martin Asks about God," "Who Is Santa Claus?" and "Children's Day at the Church" in volume 3. Generally, Sophia believed that it was unwise to introduce young children to traditional theological concepts and heritage materials until they were developmentally ready for such abstractions at about age seven.

Won't You Miss Me? and *A House for James* by Esther Bailey (1965), *Poems to Grow On* by Jean McKee Thompson (1957), and *Enjoy These Books with Children* by Josephine Gould (1965) supplemented the *Martin and Judy* series for young children. A book of songs compiled by Edith Lovell Thomas called *Martin and Judy Songs* was added to the *Martin and Judy* series in 1948.

A book of songs and readings for children, youth, and adults, called *We Sing of Life*, edited by Vincent Silliman and Irving Lowens, was published in 1955.[44] While the world raged with war in 1941 and 1942, the Department of Education emphasized the opposite with the "Gift of Life" series: *Animal Babies* by Alice Pratt, *A Brand New Baby* by Margaret Stanger, and *Growing Bigger* by Elizabeth Manwell and Sophia Fahs. I remember the stir that *Animal Babies* created at my childhood church, the Grace Universalist Church of Lowell, Massachusetts. Imagine! Teaching sex education to young children! Of course, Sophia interpreted such books as deeply religious, saying that they were about "the joy and the power and the miracle of being alive."[45]

Joseph: The Story of Twelve Brothers by Florence Klaber, for children ages seven through nine, and *Moses: Egyptian Prince, Nomad Sheikh, Lawgiver* by John W. Flight, for children ages nine through twelve, were published in 1941 and 1942. Sophia tried and tried to get someone with a scholarly knowledge of the New Testament to write a book on Jesus but finally decided to do it herself. In 1943 she brought a few chapters to the Curriculum Committee and passed them out anonymously, as was the custom with prospective curricula, asking for criticism. The Committee was delighted by the unknown author's work. The only criticism came from Duncan Howlett, who suggested that the author tried too hard to make the story realistic by adding details about life in Bible times known to scholars but not in the Bible.[46] After that meeting, Ernest Kuebler escorted Sophia to her taxi and asked, "Who wrote that thing on Jesus?" As she waved good-bye, she said with a smile: "I did!"[47] Thus was born *Jesus: The Carpenter's Son* (1945), one of the more popular books in the New Beacon Series for upper elementary and junior high children.

Who Do Men Say That I Am? by Susanna Wilder, a more advanced book on the life of Jesus for older teens, designed to help them use the tools of modern Biblical scholars, was added to the New Beacon Series in 1965.

Some books never became popular. For example, a 1940 book of value-centered stories for junior high youth called *Nothing Ever Happens and How It Does,* by Dorothy Canfield Fisher and Sarah N. Cleghorn, did not sell well and was dropped from the catalogue by the mid-1940s.[48]

Building on the old popular Beacon Course book *God's Wonder World* and an experimental course on science and religion for children at Riverside Church, Sophia organized a series of leaflets for children and an adult guide book called *How Miracles Abound,* by Bertha Stevens, which were ready for use by 1943.[49] She added to the materials a series of worship services for children on the various natural wonders studied in the curriculum: magnets, stars, water, birds' nests, the human hand, etc. The course became widely used and was totally redeveloped as the Beacon Science Series in the early 1960s.

By the mid-1940s, most Universalist churches were using the New Beacon Series books. In 1946 the Universalists reorganized their Department of Education and formed a committee to coordinate its services. The committee was composed of representatives from the two Universalist-founded theological schools (at Tufts College and St. Lawrence University), the General Sunday School Association, the youth group, and the Association of Universalist Women.[50] Angus MacLean was the first chair. As part of their work, they hired Alice Harrison, the director of religious education at the Universalist Church of Lynn, Massachusetts, as director of youth activities for both junior and senior high levels.[51] She organized junior high rallies and served on the staffs of numerous senior high conferences. When the Universalist Youth Fellowship (called the Young Peoples' Christian Union until 1941) and the American Unitarian Youth (called the Young Peoples' Religious Union until 1941) merged into Liberal Religious Youth in 1954, Alice became the associate director until 1957.[52] In the 1960s, Alice headed the Junior High Department of the UUA. She produced a series of pamphlets for training junior high youth group leaders and church school teachers. Her booklet entitled *Religious Education for the Junior Higher* came out in 1964 and identifies the numerous resources that were available from her office.

Edna Bruner was the field worker for the Universalists during most of the 1940s and 1950s. She drove about the continent with a trunk full of curricula, preaching with her rich contralto voice and leading numerous workshops at churches and area gatherings. The *How Miracles Abound* curriculum was one of her favorites. She always advocated an approach to religious education that involved the total church.[53] When the two denominations formed the Council of Liberal Churches in 1954, she continued her field work for both until consolidation in 1961, then became an educational consultant for the UUA until 1968.

I attended one of her workshops in the late 1950s and recall a story she told from her life. She had been given a dozen American Beauty red roses on some special occasion and brought them to her church school room on Sunday morning. She set the vase of roses down on the low table and went to the supply room to get some supplies. Somehow she was delayed by other teachers needing her help, and when she got back to her classroom she stopped at the doorway in shock! Some of the children had arrived and were standing around the table picking the roses apart. Petals were everywhere, on the table and the floor. Something deep down inside her made her hold her anger back long enough to hear what they were saying. After listening to their words of joy and watching them handle the beautiful petals, she realized *they were worshipping!* She found herself transformed by the children, from one extreme of feelings to the other, kneeling down with them, cherishing the petals, and of course, the children, as she joined in picking the roses apart. She said that that was the most meaningful worship experience she had had with young children.

As Edna Bruner and Frances Wood traveled about the continent, they heard people asking for ways to teach Unitarianism and Universalism. Stephen Fritchman's *Men of Liberty* in 1944 and Reginald Manwell and Sophia Fahs's *The Church across the Street* in 1947 helped to meet that request.[54] In 1962 Henry H. Cheetham, then the new director of the Department of Education, added to that effort with his small book, *Unitarianism and Universalism: An Illustrated History,* for teenagers. In 1964 Clinton Lee Scott further enriched the literature for teens with *These Live Tomorrow: Twenty Unitarian Universalist Biographies.*

The most long-lasting book of the New Beacon Series came out in 1945: *From Long Ago and Many Lands* by Sophia Fahs. It clearly expressed the goal of encouraging a world-centered view of religion with its Chinese theme, "Under the sky, all people are one family." It was not only used for children from ages seven to nine in church school, but grew to be popular with storytellers beyond that context. Commenting at the back of the book on the three birth stories of Jesus, Buddha, and Confucius, Sophia wrote that they should "remind us that long ago people loved newborn babies as much as we do, and felt that nothing could be too wonderful to have happened to a baby that grew to be a good and noble person."[55]

Somewhat in contrast, three more Bible-centered books, with teaching guides, were published: *The Drama of Ancient Israel* by

John W. Flight (1949), *Men of Prophetic Fire* by Rolland Wolfe (1950), and *The Old Story of Salvation* by Sophia Fahs (1955). I recall them all being used in most of our churches, but it took an unusually dynamic teacher, knowledgeable about the needs of young people, to make any of them come alive.

The 1950s also produced *The Family Finds Out* by Edith Hunter (1951), for five- and six-year-olds; *The Tuckers, Growing to Know Themselves* by Katherine Wensberg (1952), for primary-age children; and several books for teens: *War's Unconquered Children Speak* by Alice Cobb (1953), *Socrates: The Man Who Dared to Ask* by Cora Mason (1953), *Peace and War: Man-Made* by Tom Gait (1952), and *Questions That Matter Most: Asked by the World's Religions* by Floyd Ross and Tynette Hills (1954). It is my impression that *The Family Finds Out* and *The Tuckers* were used widely. Of the others, only *Questions That Matter Most was used to any extent, and that somewhat moderately. In 1966 Katherine Wensberg authored another book for the series, *Experiences with Living Things: An Introduction to Ecology for Five-to-Eight-Year-Olds.* As the title indicates, it helped teachers provide an experience-centered program for children to help them develop their own philosophy of life by observing small animals and plants in their classroom and exploring the natural settings around their church buildings.

In the spring of 1949, Sophia Fahs, Ernest Kuebler, and Frances Wood founded the Unitarian professional organization for liberal religious educators. They personally invited a number of employed directors of religious education to a week-long conference at Chautauqua, New York, with Sophia as the key program leader. Out of a meeting on June 23 at that conference and a follow-up meeting at Star Island a few weeks later emerged the Unitarian Education Directors' Association (UEDA). Jean Humphreys (Cochran) of Wellesley Hills, Massachusetts, was chosen as the first president. In 1955 the name was changed to the Liberal Religious Education Directors Association (LREDA), so that Universalists and other professional liberal religious educators could feel fully included. (For further information, see *Giving Birth to Ourselves: A History of the Liberal Religious*

Educators Association, 1949-1999 by Joan W. Goodwin, published by LREDA in 1999.)

In 1954 Edith Hunter, Lucile Lindberg, and Dorothy Spoerl were hired as part-time editors by the Council of Liberal Churches. Robert L'H. Miller joined their ranks in 1956. Ernest Kuebler continued to head the reorganized Division of Education until the Unitarian Universalist consolidation in 1961. In that period, Edith Hunter wrote her *Conversations with Children* (1961), a book containing interviews with six- and seven-year-olds, intended for adults to read and discuss with children. Also, Dorothy Spoerl edited *Tensions Our Children Live With* (1959), a collection of stories about children from a variety of family backgrounds ("broken homes," racial and cultural minorities, etc.) and intended to be used with grades three through six. Nearly all of the leaders in religious education circles knew of and appreciated these books in the 1950s and early 1960s, but with the exception of *Conversations with Children*, they did not have a wide appeal among the congregations. An earlier book by Raymond B. Johnson, *What Is Happening in Religious Education*, discussed the philosophy of the New Beacon Series up to 1948. It was popular in the late 1940s and early 1950s but was dropped from later lists of materials when more books in the series were published.

Sophia retired in 1951 at age seventy-five, but she agreed to serve as curriculum consultant into the mid-1960s.[56] Her monumental work, *Today's Children and Yesterday's Heritage: A Philosophy of Creative Religious Development*, was published in 1952 and became the most important pedagogical work on teaching heritage material for the Fahs/MacLean Era. Angus MacLean wrote the introduction and religious educators used it throughout the movement, especially to help themselves and others discover how to use traditional materials with children. The book was in its fourth printing by 1954; and even today, some of us hand it to an outstanding teacher or parent, knowing that we lack something more up-to-date to give them that is of comparable quality.

A hidden gem from Sophia's pen is *Worshipping Together with Questioning Minds*, published in 1965. If you really want to know how she faced the challenge of being fully with children while encouraging their growing spirituality, I recommend you read that book. Elizabeth Anastos called Sophia "a monistic, natural theist."[57] It was a challenge to be that kind of believer and lead children's worship using a participatory process. The book's jacket elaborates what she tried to share: "How to awaken in children wondering awareness and reverent thinking, especially about invisible and intangible realities." In essence, because Ultimate Reality is indefinable, one of the best ways to worship with children is to deepen their questions and help them appreciate life and the universe with wonder and awe.

Sophia was ordained in 1959 at age eighty-two, at what is now called the Cedar Lane Unitarian Universalist Church of Bethesda, Maryland. By that time, she was already regarded as a legend in her own time. True to form, she preached her own ordination sermon, calling for higher professional standards and more organized research in religious education. Edith Hunter's moving biography of her life, published seven years later, continued to build her legendary influence on our movement and remains an important source of the history of liberal religious education.

David B. Parke wrote one of the best tributes to Sophia in his doctoral dissertation, *The Historical and Religious Antecedents of the New Beacon Series in Religious Education*:

> The new Beacon Series in Religious Education emerged out of, and was a synthesis of, the liberal movement in theology, the progressive movement in education, and the critical movement in Biblical studies. In the figure of Sophia Lyon Fahs, the synthesis found articulation at precisely the moment when the American Unitarians were seeking a curriculum editor. The appointment of Mrs. Fahs in 1937 was the crucial event in the modern history of Unitarian religious education. In its way it was more important than Channing's address on the Sunday School in 1837, for whereas Channing only announced a revolution, Mrs. Fahs effected one.[58]

Turning to adult religious education, it is important to realize that the Unitarian movement was growing during the post-

World War II period. Between 1947 and 1957, adult membership had increased 53 percent, from approximately 69,104 to 106,000, and church school enrollment had increased 169 percent, from 17,099 to 46,000.[59] In part this was due to the general growth of religious groups in that period, but it is quite probable that the growth in church school enrollment was also due to the high quality of religious education programs led by well-trained professionals and teachers.

A special aspect of this growth was the development of *fellowships*, small groups of laypeople who had discovered Unitarianism and lived in areas where no Unitarian churches existed. At first that growth was spontaneous, but the AUA soon hired layperson Munroe Husbands to facilitate the process and organize additional fellowships. From 1947 to 1957, 216 new fellowships were developed.[60] The American Unitarian Association in the late 1940s and early 1950s, the Council of Liberal Churches (CLC) in the late 1950s, and the UUA in the 1960s used their adult education staff, Merrill Bush (1946-1950) and Royal Cloyd (1957-1968), to develop program materials for the fellowships.[61] William Y. Bell, probably the first African American to head a denominational program section, was in charge of adult education and social relations for the CLC in 1954, but health problems forced him to resign before he had completed a year's service.[62]

Some adult education materials of the period were directed more to established churches than fellowships, but both used them. Among those materials were the Ten Days for Celebration series, designed to help ministers plan various holiday services; the At Issue series on social action; and the Beacon 25 series of tapes and guides for discussion groups.[63]

In the earlier part of the Fahs/MacLean Era, one example of an adult education program was a series of booklets for discussion groups called *The Helper*, published by the Universalist Publishing House. Each issue of *The Helper* had a theme. For example, volume 72, no. 3 in 1941 was entitled "Lifting Life to a Religious Level: Studies in Religious Faith and Experience." Some of the chapter headings were "Shall We Still Put Our Trust in Religion?" "Affirmations and Beliefs Which Are Not

Outmoded," "Our Materialistic Culture," "Prejudices," and "The Christian Personality."

During the Fahs/MacLean Era, the spheres of adult religious education and children's religious education were separate but overlapping. Although most directors of religious education did not consider adult programming as part of their job description, some did. Both program spheres comprised the bulk of the work of the Council of Liberal Churches before consolidation, and the leaders of both spheres knew each other. Field workers Edna Bruner and Frances Wood included both kinds of materials in their presentations to churches and fellowships, but they probably channeled the adult program materials more toward ministers and presidents of fellowships and the children's materials more toward directors of religious education and chairs of religious education committees. Among the curriculum writers, Dorothy Spoerl was an important link between the two spheres. She wrote for both and switched to the adult education staff of the new Unitarian Universalist Association in the 1960s.

The adult education goals of the writers of the New Beacon Series included the development of materials for parents. In the early 1960s, a series of attractive pamphlets, specifically written for parents, was produced for the various curricula then in use. Most directors of religious education gave the pamphlets to parents as they registered their children for church school.

Before concluding this paper, it is important to give an overview of the New Beacon Series. Two contrasting studies by Robert L'H. Miller and Dorothy Spoerl are instructive.

In 1957 Robert Miller did an extensive study of the New Beacon Series for his doctor of theology degree in religious education at Boston University. He was teaching religious education at Crane Theological School of Tufts University at the time. His analysis revealed that although the writers and field workers of the New Beacon Series frequently advocated a progressive education philosophy, most of the materials produced were not really experience-centered and child-centered but rather content-centered and teacher-centered, especially in the curricula for older children and adolescents. Even the curricula for younger children focused on stories about the experiences of others rather than on the direct experiences of the children. The curricula for older children and youth were predominantly based on the Bible and world religions and written to reflect a liberal religious view. Activities, such as dramatizations, were designed to help students learn that view. In his conclusion, Miller called for the development of a unified philosophy of religious education for the Council of Liberal Churches and advocated "a radical revision of the teacher's guides" with more focus on the growing experiences of young people in their own lives, a broader approach to the study of religious beliefs and traditions, and more democratic structuring of agendas in classrooms.[64]

Miller's study was shared with the Curriculum Committee of the Council of Liberal Churches, and although it did not lead to the results he had hoped for, it may have been an important influence that paved the way for the more person-centered curricula of the next era of our religious education heritage under the leadership of Hugo Hollerorth.

Toward the end of the Fahs/MacLean Era, in 1962, Dorothy Spoerl wrote a paper on the New Beacon Series in which she compared it with previous curricula, especially its immediate predecessor, the Beacon Course (1915-1935). Her purpose was to point out the advances that had been made in curriculum development and to emphasize that the writers of the New Beacon Series viewed their books, guides, and other materials as an ongoing process, always to be added to as an expanding body of resources for teachers, parents, and young people, and open to continuing research and revision.[65]

Spoerl noted that, while previous curricula had included some elements of nature study, modern science, and world religions, there was a change in theology in the New Beacon Series. Human nature appeared to be "separated from God" in the old but was viewed as "bound together with God" in the new.[66] The new curricula had no rigid separation between the sacred and secular. Children's natural experiences and their growing processes and questioning minds were seen as containing within them the essence of religion.

Spoerl also pointed out that the Curriculum Committee had drawn to its ranks top authorities in psychology and education and used their collective wisdom to improve the teachers' guides and teacher-training programs. Where the old curricula had emphasized question-and-answer lessons, workbooks with pictures to color, and puzzles, the new guides suggested many more varied activities. The children's books had better illustrations, and many more supportive materials, such as films and records. She reaffirmed the influence of progressive education on curricula and concluded, "teachers and children together, growing into an awareness of the spiritual meanings of living — this is the genius of the New Beacon Series in Religious Education."[67]

The contrast between Robert Miller's and Dorothy Spoerl's views of the New Beacon Series helps us shape questions about our work in religious education. It is clear that both endorsed the experience-centered and person-centered approach to religious education advanced in progressive education theory. Miller pointed out that in actual practice the curriculum writers only approached the use of the theory in programs for young children. Spoerl pointed out that the writers had made real progress toward using the theory compared to former years, and suggested that there was a shift in theology from belief in an external God to belief in an immanent God.

Was the goal of applying progressive education theory during the Fahs/MacLean era helpful or doable? Does that goal continue after the Fahs/MacLean era? Also, how have various theological beliefs motivated our curriculum development processes? As we shape our questions and explore their implications together, we may be preparing our movement for a new era in religious education.

In closing, I wish to share with you a quote from Dorothy Spoerl's acceptance speech when she received the Angus Mac-Lean Award in 1994: "The fact is that we have to accept that the nature of what we choose to call 'truth' is constantly changing

... We can only say that this is how we arrive at today's answer, changing yesterday's, and waiting to see what the answer of tomorrow will be."[68]

NOTES

[1] Angus H. MacLean, *Parent Education in Liberal Churches*. A report to the Unitarian Church of Cleveland, Ohio, probably written in the summer of 1961, with limited distribution by the church.

[2] The Channing-Murray Group had in it about twenty-five undergraduate students attending St. Lawrence University during the late 1950s and early 1960s. The members held weekly meetings in the lounge of the theological school and attended an annual retreat with liberal religious young adults from other colleges and universities of upstate New York. Orloff W. Miller was the denominational staff person in Boston in charge of coordinating college centers during that period.

[3] For information about the history of the religious education training programs at St. Lawrence and Tufts, see Russell E. Miller, *The Larger Hope*, vol. 2, *The Second Century of the Universalist Church in America, 1870-1970* (Boston: UUA, 1985), 281-338. Those two theological schools, which closed in 1965 and 1968, respectively, were the only seminaries in the Unitarian Universalist movement offering full professional training in religious education until the recent development of the Modified Residency Program and other programs at Meadville/Lombard Theological School.

[4] Frank E. Robertson, "Sophia Fahs' Dream of a Center for Religious Education," *Liberal Religious Education* (Spring 1993), 22-29.

[5] Edith Hunter, *Sophia Lyon Fahs: A Biography* (Boston: Beacon Press, 1966), 69, 151.

[6] Eugene B. Navias, "Angus Hector MacLean," unpublished obituary written November 18, 1969.

[7] Hunter, *Sophia Lyon Fahs*, 49.

[8] Navias, "Angus Hector MacLean."

[9] Hunter, *Sophia Lyon Fahs*, 78.

[10] Hunter, *Sophia Lyon Fahs*, 88.

[11] Angus H. MacLean, *The Method Is the Message* (Boston: UUA, 1962), 15. Originally given as an address before the Universalist Sabbath School Union of Greater Boston in 1951 and subsequently rewritten for publication. The curricula referred to are: Florence Klaber, *Joseph: The Story of Twelve Brothers* (Boston: Becon Press, 1941) and John Flight, *The Drama of Ancient Israel* (Boston: Beacon Press, 1949).

[12] Richard Gilbert, "Memorial Service for Angus H. MacLean," November 17, 1969 (Ithaca, NY: First Unitarian Church of Ithaca, 1969), 4.

[13] Hunter, *Sophia Lyon Fahs*, 58-60.

[14] Interview with Verna Carncross, June, 1998.

[15] Hunter, *Sophia Lyon Fahs*, 191.

[16] Hunter, *Sophia Lyon Fahs*, 192.

[17] Hunter, *Sophia Lyon Fahs*, 192.

[18] Helen Zidowecki, "Curriculum: The Course of Life — Meet Dorothy Spoerl" (paper written for the Modified Residency Program of Meadville/Lombard Theological School, December 1, 1995).

[19] Hunter, *Sophia Lyon Fahs*, 192; but see also Dorothy Tilden Spoerl, *Unitarian Curriculum Development in the Twentieth Century* (Boston: Department of Education of the UUA, 1962).

[20] Hunter, *Sophia Lyon Fahs*, 193.

[21] Miller, *The Larger Hope* vol. 2, 213-214.

[22] Miller, *The Larger Hope* vol. 2, 210.

[23] Miller, *The Larger Hope* vol. 2, 210.

[24] American Unitarian Association Commission of Appraisal, *Unitarians Face a New Age* (Boston: AUA, 1936), 8.

[25] Summary of the report of the curriculum study committee, in Hunter, *Sophia Lyon Fahs*, 196.

[26] Hunter, *Sophia Lyon Fahs*, 197.

[27] Hunter, *Sophia Lyon Fahs*, 210.

[28] Hunter, *Sophia Lyon Fahs*, 202.

[29] Hunter, *Sophia Lyon Fahs*, 202.

[30] Zidowecki, "Curriculum: The Course of Life," 3.

[31] Sophia Fahs and Dorothy Spoerl, *Beginnings of Life And Death* (Boston: Beacon Press, 1938), 147.

[32] Hunter, *Sophia Lyon Fahs*, 122.

[33] Mildred Lester and Lucile Lindberg, *Exploring Beginnings — A Guide to Beginnings: Earth, Sky, Life, Death* (Boston: Beacon Press, 1960), preface. This guide is in hard cover and contains 136 pages.

[34] Hunter, *Sophia Lyon Fahs*, 213.

[35] Hunter, *Sophia Lyon Fahs*, 212.

[36] Zidowecki, "Curriculum: The Course of Life," 3.

[37] Hunter, *Sophia Lyon Fahs*, 212.

[38] Hunter, *Sophia Lyon Fahs*, 212.

[39] Hunter, *Sophia Lyon Fahs*, 211.

[40] Hunter, *Sophia Lyon Fahs*, 214.

[41] Hunter, *Sophia Lyon Fahs*, 215.

[42] Hunter, *Sophia Lyon Fahs*, 216.

[43] See the foreword to Josephine Gould, *Martin and Judy for Parents and Teachers* (Boston: Beacon Press, 1958).

[44] *We Sing of Life* (Boston: Beacon Press, 1955). Copyrighted by the American Ethical Union, published by Starr King Press, and distributed by Beacon Press. Sophia Fahs wrote the foreword. Florence Klaber and Algernon Black of the American Ethical Union wrote the introduction.

[45] Hunter, *Sophia Lyon Fahs*, 220.

[46] Hunter, *Sophia Lyon Fahs*, 231.

[47] Interview with Eugene Navias, September 1999.

[48] Hunter, *Sophia Lyon Fahs*, 221.

[49] Hunter, *Sophia Lyon Fahs*, 220, 221.

[50] Miller, *The Larger Hope* vol. 2, 628.

[51] I have fond memories of serving on the staff with Alice at the junior high Camp Seabreeze at Ferry Beach in the mid-1950s. She preached my ordination sermon in 1962. Alice was a vibrant, outgoing person who always accentuated the positive. She called her workshops with junior high youth "Mirror Magic" and helped them deal with their identity concerns. I also discovered that she got up early every day for private meditation; she called this time her "hour of power."

[52] Miller, *The Larger Hope* vol. 2, 207-208.

[53] Eugene B. Navias, "Once upon a Time: The Story of Edna Bruner," sermon preached at a memorial service for her at the UUA on November 18, 1997. Edna died on August 3, 1997.

[54] Hugo Hollerorth, *The Beacon Series in Religious Education* (Boston: Department of Education of the UUA, 1966), 21. Note that the word *new* was dropped from the name of the series toward the end of the era.

[55] Sophia Fahs, *From Long Ago and Many Lands* (Boston: Beacon Press, 1959), 177.

[56] Hunter, *Sophia Lyon Fahs*, 238.

[57] Elizabeth Anastos, *Unitarian Universalist Religious Education: A Brief History* (Boston: UUA, 1981), 5.

[58] David B. Parke, "The Historical and Religious Antecedents of the New Beacon Series in Religious Education" (Ph.D. diss., Boston University,

1965), quoted in Carol R. Morris, "It Was Noontime Here . . ." in *A Stream of Light: A Short History of American Unitarianism*, ed. Conrad Wright (Boston: UUA, 1985), 134.

[59] Morris, "It Was Noontime Here . . .", 149.

[60] Morris, "It Was Noontime Here . . .", 149.

[61] Interview with Royal Cloyd, September 1999.

[62] Interviews with Royal Cloyd and with Martha (Pat) Smith, an administrative assistant during the late 1950s and 1960s. Also see Miller, *The Larger Hope* vol. 2, 652, and *The Universalist Leader* (December 1954), 290.

[63] Interview with Royal Cloyd.

[64] Robert L'Hommedieu Miller, "The Educational Philosophy of the New Beacon Series in Religious Education" (thesis, Th.D. in religious education, Boston University, 1957).

[65] Spoerl, *Unitarian Curriculum Development*, 13.

[66] Spoerl, *Unitarian Curriculum Development*, 15-16.

[67] Spoerl, *Unitarian Curriculum Development*, 16.

[68] Zidowecki, "Curriculum: The Course of Life," Appendix B.

BIBLIOGRAPHY

Dozens of books, booklets, and pamphlets on religious education were printed during the Fahs/MacLean Era, extending the work of the curriculum writers. Only those works mentioned in this paper are listed here.

Anastos, Elizabeth. *Unitarian Universalist Religious Education: A Brief History.* Boston: UUA, 1981.

Cobb, Cora Stanwood. *God's Wonder World.* Boston: Beacon Press, 1918.

Dewey, John. *The Child and the Curriculum.* Chicago: University of Chicago Press, 1902.

———. *Democracy and Education: An Introduction to the Philosophy of Education.* New York: Macmillan, 1916.

Fahs, Sophia L. *The Beginnings of Mysticism in Children's Growth.* Boston: UUA, 1960.

———. *Developing Concepts of God with Children.* Boston: UUA, 1959.

———. *A New Ministry to Children.* Boston: UUA, 1960.

———. *Why Teach Religion in an Age of Science?* Boston: UUA, 1960.

Gilbert, Richard. "Memorial Service for Angus H. MacLean." Ithaca, NY: First Unitarian Church of Ithaca, 1969.

Goodwin, Joan W. *Giving Birth to Ourselves: A History of the Liberal Religious Educators Association, 1949-1999.* LREDA, 1999.

Gould, Josephine. *Enjoy These Books with Children.* Boston: Beacon Press, 1965.

Harrison, Alice M. *Religious Education for the Junior Higher.* Boston: UUA, 1964.

Hollerorth, Hugo. *The Beacon Series in Religious Education* [catalogue of church school curricula, youth programs, etc.] Boston: UUA, 1966.

Hunter, Edith. *Sophia Lyon Fahs: A Biography.* Boston: Beacon Press, 1966.

MacLean, Angus H. *The Method Is the Message.* Boston: UUA, 1962.

———. *The New Era in Religious Education: A Manual for Church School Teachers.* Boston: Beacon Press, 1934.

———. *Parent Education in Liberal Churches.* Cleveland: Unitarian Church of Cleveland, 1961.

———. *Planning the Religious Education Curriculum: Some Basic Considerations.* Boston: Department of Education of the Universalist Church of America and the American Unitarian Association, 1951.

———. *The Wind in Both Ears.* Boston: Beacon Press, 1965.

Miller, Robert L'H. "The Educational Philosophy of the New Beacon Series in Religious Education." Thesis, Th.D. in religious education, Boston University, 1957.

Miller, Russell E. *The Larger Hope.* Vol. 2, *The Second Century of the Universalist Church of America, 1870-1970.* Boston: UUA, 1985.

Navias, Eugene B. "Angus Hector MacLean" [unpublished obituary, November 18, 1969].

———. "Once upon a Time: The Story of Edna Bruner." Boston: UUA, 1997.

Robertson, Frank E. "Sophia Fahs' Dream of a Center for Religious Education." *Liberal Religious Education* (Spring 1993).

Silliman, Vincent and Irving Lowens. *We Sing of Life.* Boston: Beacon Press, 1955.

Spoerl, Dorothy T. *Unitarian Curriculum Development in the Twentieth Century.* Boston: UUA, 1962.

Wright, Conrad, ed. *A Stream of Light: A Short History of American Unitarianism.* Boston: UUA, 1985.

Zidowecki, Helen. "Curriculum: The Course of Life — Meet Dorothy Spoerl." Paper written for the Modified Residency Program of Meadville/Lombard Theological School, Chicago, 1995.

APPENDIX

PUBLICATIONS IN THE NEW BEACON SERIES (1937-1966)

All titles in this series were published by Beacon Press, Boston.

For Three- to Five-Year-Olds

Martin and Judy in Their Two Little Houses (vol. 1), Verna Hills (Bayley), 1939.

Martin and Judy in Sunshine and Rain (vol. 2), Verna Hills (Bayley) and Sophia Fahs, 1940.

Martin and Judy Playing and Learning (vol. 3), Verna Hills (Bayley), 1943.

Early Teachers' Guides for the *Martin and Judy* series were written by Dorothy Spoerl, Margaret Price, and Elizabeth Manwell.

Martin and Judy Songs, compiled by Edith Lovell Thomas, 1948.

Martin and Judy: for Parents and Teachers, Josephine T. Gould, 1951.

Poems to Grow On, Jean McKee Thompson, 1957 (also used for older children).

A House for James, Esther Bailey, 1965.

Won't You Miss Me? Esther Bailey, 1965.

For Five- to Seven-Year-Olds

The Family Finds Out, Edith Hunter, 1951.

Exploring Nature and Life with Five- and Six-Year-Olds (Guide to *The Family Finds Out*), Edith Hunter, 1951.

For Eight- and Nine-Year-Olds

Child of the Sun: A Pharaoh Of Egypt, Margaret Dulles Edwards, 1939.

Guide to *Child Of The Sun*, Margaret Dulles Edwards, 1940.

Joseph: The Story of Twelve Brothers, Florence W. Klaber, 1941.

Guide to *Joseph*, Florence W. Klaber, 1941.

How Miracles Abound, Bertha Stevens, 1941.

Guide to *How Miracles Abound*, Dorothy Irma Cooke, Jeanette Perkins Brown, and Sophia L. Fahs, 1943.

Leading Children in Worship (ten services on themes from *How Miracles Abound*), Sophia L. Fahs, 1943.

From Long Ago and Many Lands, Sophia L. Fahs, 1948.

Guide to *From Long Ago And Many Lands*, Florence W. Klaber.

For Ten- to Twelve-Year-Olds

Beginnings of Earth And Sky, Sophia L. Fahs, 1937.

Beginnings of Life And Death, Sophia L. Fahs and Dorothy T. Spoerl, 1938.

Guides to both *Beginnings* books, Sophia L. Fahs and Mildred Tenny, 1938, 1939.

Moses: Egyptian Prince, Nomad Sheikh, Lawgiver, John W. Flight, 1942.

Guide to *Moses*, Edna L. Acheson and Sophia L. Fahs, 1942.

Jesus: The Carpenter's Son, Sophia L. Fahs, 1945.

Guide to *Jesus: The Carpenter's Son*, Sophia L. Fahs, 1945.

Beginnings: Earth, Sky, Life, Death, Sophia L. Fahs and Dorothy T. Spoerl, 1958.

Exploring Beginnings — A Guide to Beginnings: Earth, Sky, Life, Death, Mildred Lester and Lucile Lindberg, 1960.

For Twelve-Year-Olds and Teens

The Church across the Street, Reginald D. Manwell and Sophia L. Fahs, 1947 (revised in 1962).

Guide to *The Church across the Street*, Reginald D. Manwell and Sophia Fahs, 1947.

The Drama of Ancient Israel, John W. Flight, 1949.

Guide to *The Drama Of Ancient Israel*, Elsie M. Bush.

The Old Story Of Salvation (guide included), Sophia L. Fahs, 1955.

For Teens

Primitive Faiths, workbook and guide by Elizabeth MacDonald, 1937.

Hinduism, workbook and guide by Elizabeth MacDonald, 1938.

Men of Liberty: Ten Unitarian Pioneers, Stephen H. Fritchman, 1944.

Men of Prophetic Fire, Rolland Emerson Wolfe, 1951.

Guide to *Men Of Prophetic Fire*, Marguerite Ashbrook, Elizabeth G. Sprague, and Wayne Shuttee, 1952.

Peace and War: Man-Made, Tom Galt, 1952.

War's Unconquered Children Speak, Alice Cobb, 1953.

Socrates: The Man Who Dared to Ask, Cora Mason, 1953.

Guide to *Socrates*, Doreen Spitzer, 1954.

Questions That Matter Most: Asked by the World's Religions, Floyd H. Ross and Tynette W. Hills, 1954.

Guide to *Questions That Matter Most*, Floyd H. Ross and Tynette W. Hills.

Abraham: His Heritage and Ours, Dorothy Hill, 1957.

Unitarianism and Universalism: An Illustrated History, Henry H. Cheetham, 1962.
These Live Tomorrow: Twenty Unitarian Universalist Biographies, Clinton Lee Scott, 1964.
Who Do Men Say That I Am? Susanna Wilder Heinz, 1965.
Guide to *Who Do Men Say That I Am?* Charles C. Forman, 1966.

The Gift of Life Series

Animal Babies, Alice Day Pratt, 1941.
A Brand New Baby, Margaret A. Stanger, 1942.
Growing Bigger, Elizabeth M. Manwell and Sophia L. Fahs, 1942.
The Gift of Life: A Guide for Teachers and Parents, Josephine T. Gould, Dorothy T. Spoerl, and Elizabeth M. Manwell, 1942.
The Tuckers: Growing To Know Themselves, Katherine Wensberg and Mary Myrle Northrop (guide bound in), 1952.
Always Growing, Elizabeth M. Manwell, 1957.
Teaching Primary Children (a guide to the Gift of Life Series), Josephine T. Gould, Lucile Lindberg, and Jannette Spitzer, 1957.
Experiences with Living Things: An Introduction to Ecology for Five-to-Eight-Year-Olds, Katherine Wensberg, 1966.

The Beacon Science Series

The Endless Sky, E. Marie Boyle, 1961.
Flowers – Carriers of Life, E. Marie Boyle, 1961.
The Leafy Home of the Birds, E. Marie Boyle, 1961.
Magnets, Caroline and Kendrick Fenderson, Jr., 1961.
New England Shores, Hildreth Shaw Frost, 1961.
Rocks That Captured History, Edith C. Kingsbury, 1961.
Water: Its Form and Motion, E. Marie Boyle, 1961.
Hands, Dorothy T. Spoerl, probably 1961.
Bees, Margaret Ritchie, 1964.
Microorganisms: Little Plants and Animals, Mabel Ruttle, 1964.
The Migrating Birds, Janet E. Givens, 1964.
Seedless Plants – Soil Builders, E. Marie Boyle, 1964.
Southern Shores, Caroline and Kendrick Fenderson, Jr., 1964.
The Web Weavers, D. Irma Cooke, 1964.
What Is Real, Josephine and Lawrence Gould, 1964.
The Wonderful Heart, Hellen Goudsmit, 1964.

Sample Parents' Guides

For parents of children studying:
  Martin and Judy, Elizabeth Williams (light pink), 1963.
  The Beacon Science Series, Pauline S. Gilson (grey), 1963.
  From Long Ago and Many Lands, Louise H. Stuart (yellow), 1963.
  Moses, Eugene B. Navias (white), 1963.

Books on the Philosophy of the New Beacon Series

Consider the Children: How They Grow, Elizabeth M. Manwell and Sophia L. Fahs (a focus on the *Martin and Judy* series), 1940.

What Is Happening in Religious Education, Raymond B. Johnson, 1948.

Today's Children and Yesterday's Heritage: A Philosophy of Creative Religious Development, Sophia L. Fahs, 1952.

The Questioning Child and Religion, Edith F. Hunter, 1956.

Tensions Our Children Live With (thirty-three stories for nine- to eleven year-olds), edited by Dorothy T. Spoerl, 1959.

Conversations with Children (six- to ten-year-olds), Edith F. Hunter, 1961.

Worshipping Together with Questioning Minds, Sophia L. Fahs, 1965.

Hugo J. Hollerorth

AN ERA OF CHANGE 1965-1980

In the opening paragraph of his monumental study of the 1960s in four Western societies — the United States, England, France, and Italy — the British historian Arthur Marwick states,

> Mention of "the sixties" rouses strong emotions even in those who were already old when the sixties began and those who were not even born when the sixties ended. For some it is a golden age, for others a time when the old secure framework of morality, authority, and discipline disintegrated. In the eyes of the far left, it is the era when revolution was at hand, only to be betrayed by the feebleness of the faithful and the trickery of the enemy; to the radical right, an era of subversion and moral turpitude.[1]

If the 1960s represented a golden age for some in the broader culture and the disintegration of morality and discipline to others, so it was also in our own Unitarian Universalist religious community. We had our own upheavals in the 1960s, which paralleled closely those in the broader culture: an internal civil rights struggle with the 1969 General Assembly granting a form of empowerment to a segment of our black membership that some UUs saw as the antithesis of liberalism's vision of racial integration and cooperation; a youth sub-culture that tugged and pushed against our institutional norms, questioning their authenticity at every point; the dismissal by many of our Judeo-

51

Christian roots and the search for a religious orientation for the human adventure in Eastern religions; massive experimentation in personal relationships and sexual behavior explored through encounter groups, "T" groups, sensitivity training, nonverbal communication workshops, and a myriad of other forms of personal and group encounters; a distrust of institutions, including religious organizations (even the UUA was suspect!); the new feminism, which had to struggle mightily for a foothold in what was then (and maybe still is) a male-dominated religious institution; and the gay liberation movement, which had to struggle even harder than the feminist movement in the face of some major UU leaders' belief that homosexuality was a psychiatric disorder. All of this took place within the context of an optimism and genuine faith in the dawning of a new world. It was an audacious, defiant, exhilarating time. As in the broader culture, some UUs thought it was the dawning of a much-needed revolutionary era within our religious community that was eventually betrayed by the feebleness of the faithful and a retreat to middle-class respectability. Others interpreted much of what happened in the 1960s as UUs acting out a delayed adolescence and were relieved when, as they saw it, we moved on in the 1980s to become a more spiritually mature community.[2]

It was within this cultural and UU institutional context that the decision was made to develop new religious education curricula for our churches and fellowships. Some of the introductory material for teachers and parents in the very first program in the new series acknowledged the milieu in which we were living. The curriculum, titled *Decision Making*, was developed to help preadolescent boys and girls become imaginative and responsible decision makers. In the introduction for teachers and parents, the authors, Clyde and Barbara Dodder, wrote:

> The tide has gone out on a lot of things that used to seem very durable, very unchanging. Among the goods left washed ashore it is possible to distinguish the remains of a morality ethics that was thought to be universally applicable, infallible, capable of

codification. And it's both embarrassing and disturbing to see its skeleton exposed.

We live in a time distinguished by the experience of being pushed in a multitude of directions. And if we begin asking "What's right?" and "What's wrong?" and "Why?" about private decisions or societal actions, we can feel the stress increase in a special personal way ...

New ethical patterns are being born. And they have fallout in unexpected changes in attitude, synthesis of understanding, or creation of fresh behavior idioms. Out of a multitude of apparently disconnected ways of acting and responding will emerge a mosaic of which someday, someone will say, "It means ..." and we will reply, "Yes." In the interim most people are bewildered.[3]

The children of our church and fellowship schools were thrust into the midst of this bewilderment in one of the first learning activities of the *Decision Making* curriculum. The activity, called "The Quarry Adventure,"[4] presents common moral dilemmas that often occur in real life with painful consequences. It tells the story of two best friends, Don and Andy. Don tells Andy during school on Friday that he is going to sneak away sometime over the weekend and go swimming in the abandoned rock quarry a mile south of town. He wants Andy to go with him. Both boys know that the quarry is a very dangerous place to swim. Two children were drowned there several summers ago, after which town officials urged parents to forbid their children to swim there. Both Don's and Andy's parents have been adamant about the boys not going anywhere near the quarry.

The children using *Decision Making* in our church schools were faced with immediate choices. If they were Don's best friend, would they go swimming with him in the quarry? Would they attempt to persuade Don to give up his plan? Would they tell Don's mother about his plan in order to protect the life of their best friend? Or would they do nothing? As the story progressed, the children were faced with additional choices. Early Saturday afternoon, Andy meets Don on the way to the quarry. Now he knows Don is really going there to swim and he is going alone. As Andy passes Don's house on his way to his own home, the children have to decide if he should stop and tell Don's mother.

Early Saturday evening brings the need for another decision. Don's mother calls Andy to ask if he knows Don's whereabouts. He had left home after lunch, saying he was headed to the school playground for a baseball game. When he didn't return for dinner his father drove to the playground but no one was there. Now would the children tell Don's mother where he is? He could be in trouble but maybe he has just lost track of time. In the story, Andy tells Don's mother where he is. Don's parents drive to the quarry and find him. He is fine; he has simply lost track of time. Something else is lost too — Don's freedom. Don parents ground him for a full month. In school the next day Don refuses to talk to Andy and Andy gets the same cold treatment from their mutual friends. Andy wonders what to do next and so do the children in the church school.

Two sets of symbols and a game board were provided to aid the children in trying to decide what to do at each critical point in the story. Each of the first set of symbols represented a *value* that might be important to a child and that he or she might use by itself or in connection with other values in trying to decide what to do. The values represented by the symbols were adventure, fear, loyalty, and obedience. Each of the second set of symbols represented a *person* or *thing* that a child might care about in the situation and that would be supported, threatened, or both supported and threatened by any decision he or she might make. The various persons or things represented by the symbols were the child, his or her best friend, the friend's parents, his or her own parents, and respect for authority.

As the children placed the symbols on the game board, they began to make various discoveries. Acting on the basis of any one value or combination of values may support some persons or things one cares about while it threatens others. Sometimes it is even more complex in that acting on the basis of a value or combination of values both supports *and* threatens some persons or things one cherishes. They also discovered that the values one cares about often conflict in real-life situations and one may have to violate some values in order to act on the basis of others. They discovered, too, that in any one situation, the order of importance of one's values may change as the situation changes.

The Quarry Adventure set the stage for the children to discover through a variety of learning activities a decision-making process that not only acknowledged the complexity of the Quarry situation but of the human enterprise in general. They could affirm the statement by the Dodders that when we begin asking "What's right?" and "What's wrong?" and "Why?" about private decisions or societal actions, we can feel the stress increase with every step we take.

This description of a bit of the first curriculum program in the new series is not without purpose. It provides a context for looking at some of the reasons for developing a new curriculum series beginning in the mid-1960s and continuing through the 1970s, as well as some of the critical issues, controversies, and decisions that were a part of the history of its development.

Why the Commitment to a New Curriculum Series

In 1959, the UUA appointed six study commissions to assess the crucial mission of the free church in a changing world. Even in the late 1950s, UUs were aware of the gathering forces of change that would coalesce a few years later in the 1960s. However, a reading of the reports of the commissions today suggests that we had very little inkling of the magnitude of the impending changes. Nor did we know how much *we* needed to change. Sixty-eight people were appointed to the six study commissions. Only eight of them were women!

One of the commissions was titled "Education and Liberal Religion," and it included some of the most honored names of that era in religious education: Angus MacLean, the beloved dean of the Theological School of St. Lawrence University; Robert Miller and Elizabeth Baker, long-time colleagues in the profession of religious education; Evelyn Pitcher, director of the Eliot-Pearson School at Tufts University; and myself. Irving

Murray, minister of the First Unitarian Church in Baltimore, was our chair. Paul Carnes, destined for the UUA presidency, was consultant to the Commission.

The extensive report of the Education Commission, published along with the offerings of the other Commissions in a booklet titled *The Free Church in a Changing World*, argued:

> Effective religious education for the 6-11-year-old must be based upon his needs, abilities and interests. Especially in the first three grades, his sense of personal worth requires just as much nurture as in the preschool years. But he must be given increasing opportunities for the practice of freedom within widening boundaries. His attention should be directed to the consequence of choices. Evaluation of decision-making and of action ought to be an important part of his learning.[5]

I was teaching religious education at our Theological School at St. Lawrence University in Canton, New York, during the time that I served on the Commission. Several years later, I was appointed director of curriculum development in what was then the Division of Education and Program at the UUA. The words of the Commission report were echoed in even stronger and broader terms at the first meeting of the Division of Education's Advisory Committee subsequent to my appointment. The committee set forth a mandate that the new thrust in curriculum development must stay close to the life situations of children and youth and their efforts to deal with them.

This was not a rejection of the astounding contributions of the Fahs years. However, it was a recognition that most of the Fahs-era curriculum, beyond the early elementary years, was book-centered, with the content drawn from Biblical and historical materials rather than experientially grounded in the world of children and youth. In the judgment of the Advisory Committee, this was not the focus needed for helping children orient themselves to a world where "new ethical patterns were being born with unexpected changes in attitudes, syntheses of understanding and the creation of fresh behavior idioms." Incidentally, Robert West, also destined for the UUA presidency, was chair of the Division's Advisory Committee. Dr. Henry

Cheetham was Director of the Division. Other department staff included Edna Bruner, Alice Harrison, Betty LaSalle, Dorothy Spoerl, Frances Wood, and a newly appointed young upstart like myself named Eugene Navias, who was to be a constant joy in the years ahead. The support staff included three beloved people who contributed far more than their job descriptions ever came close to describing: Lotta Hempel, Rose Muggeridge, and Ann Najarian.

Critical Issue: Models of Teaching

What were some of the critical issues, controversies and decisions that were a part of the history of developing the new curriculum series? One of the issues was what model of teaching to utilize in developing new curricula. Throughout my discussion of *Decision Making*, I used the phrase "the children discovered" and for good reasons. Henry Cheetham was a committed and learned scholar and educator in touch with the bubbling ferment occurring in educational theory at the time. He had received a long memorandum from James Gallagher and Robert Spaulding, two distinguished and valued members of our Urbana-Champaign church in Illinois. Both men taught educational theory at the University of Illinois, but also put their educational know-how to work in the Urbana-Champaign Church School.

Gallagher was a pioneer in developing what was referred to as "the discovery method" in education, while Spaulding was equally influential in formulating "the spiral method." The memorandum described in great detail how UU educational materials had fallen far behind in implementing newer and more effective educational methodologies and strategies. After I met with the two men in Urbana, they agreed to join the UUA's new efforts in curriculum development. Gallagher had already created some learning activities for a decision-making course he was teaching in the local church school. These activities provided the impetus for a team of imaginative UUs, including Gallagher, to develop the UUA's decision-making program. The team also included Milton Senn, director of the Child Study Center at Yale;

Blanche Senn, a talented religious educator in our church in New Haven; and Betty Pingal, the religious education director at the First Unitarian Society of Denver. Spaulding joined an equally imaginative team that developed the series *Man the Culture Builder, Parts I and II*. The fact that I agreed without blinking an eye to the course title *MAN the Culture Builder* and later to a course title, *MAN the Meaning Maker*, indicates how much the new director of curriculum development needed to change.

Gallagher brought his commitment to the discovery method to the development of the decision-making curriculum and proposed it as a model for the UUA's curriculum efforts. The discovery method was grounded in the conviction that the most effective learning occurs when children have an opportunity to intuit principles for themselves from concrete experiences in their daily lives. Principles developed in this way have a visceral connection with the children because they are rooted in what they have felt, tasted, smelled, seen, and heard. Thus, when we want the children to become aware of the principle that ordering values is one of the necessary steps in responsible decision making, we place them in situations in which they must choose between conflicting values. The discovery method was born out of the rejection of a kind of teaching that is always "telling" children the meaning or the importance of something without providing or trusting the kinds of learning experiences that allow a child's own understandings to emerge gradually over time.

Dr. Gallagher's introduction of the discovery method caused all of us to be more self-conscious about educational method and learning theory. Some of us eventually came to the conclusion that the discovery method was too structured. Some critics pointed out that although the teacher doesn't tell the children what to think, he or she plans and executes learning activities with an idea in mind about what the children should "discover." Some critics accused the proponents of the method of using it to manipulate children to arrive at the ideas held by the proponents. In subsequent curricula, we moved to a less structured educational model that provided more freedom for any group of participants to create different understandings from concrete experiences in their daily lives.

In the UUA's sexuality program, which I will refer to later, we used a four-stage educational model, a version of the inquiry method advocated by the School of Education at Columbia University in New York. Those of you familiar with the program will remember that the four stages were initiation, interaction, investigation, and internalization. The model affirmed the premise of the discovery method — that effective learning occurs when learners have an opportunity to intuit principles from actual experience — but it encouraged and supported more divergence. The inquiry method was also championed by Norman Benson, who became the stellar Director of the Division after the untimely death of Henry Cheetham.

Educational method has been a critical issue for UU religious educators. When Angus MacLean asserted that "the method is the message,"[6] he reminded us that a commitment to free and responsible inquiry is an integral part of our faith and that we must live this principle with our children if we want them to live and honor it in their own lives. Educational method was of critical importance in the development of the new curricula, which is why we tried to include on our curriculum teams educators who taught educational methodology in our colleges and universities as well as religious educators from our churches and fellowships.

Critical Issue: Philosophical Questions

In addition to finding ourselves involved in controversies over educational method, we were also often caught up in the philosophical controversies raging in the academic world of thought and inquiry. One example was the controversy over competing theories of the development of moral judgment — the six-stage theory set forth by Lawrence Kohlberg and the competing theory of situation ethics, perhaps expounded most eloquently by

Joseph Fletcher of Episcopal Theological Seminary in Cambridge, Massachusetts.

In Kohlberg's view, human beings move through six stages in the development of moral judgment. The development reflects the expansion in moral understanding from an individual to a societal to a universal point of view. During the first two stages, moral judgment is anchored in an ego-centrism based on individual need, such as avoiding trouble for oneself or getting something one wants. During stages three and four, it is anchored in shared norms that sustain relationships, groups, communities, and societies — norms such as helping and pleasing others and doing what important people (authorities) think is right. During stages five and six, moral judgment is anchored in what Kohlberg identifies as universal principles of justice. Reflecting on societal values but from a perspective outside that of one's own society, the individual is able to construct universally applicable moral principles based on respect for the dignity of human beings as individuals and the equality of human rights. From the perspective of these principles, the individual can arrive at objectively just (fair) resolutions of particular moral dilemmas with which all rational persons can agree. The key to a just solution is based on what Kohlberg calls the principle of reversibility. A just solution to a moral dilemma is a solution acceptable to all parties in a situation in which none of them know which role they will occupy in the situation. Thus, capital punishment is always wrong because no one in a situation would support it if he or she were the one to be put to death. Similarly, lying is always wrong because no one in a situation would want to be the one who is lied to.[7]

In contrast to Kohlberg, situation ethicists maintain that responsible moral action lies not in following an abstract set of principles but in responding to persons in particular, concrete situations. This position is in line with Martin Buber's insistence that to be responsible means to hear the *particular* call or claims of others. Maurice Friedman, in his book *Martin Buber: The Life of Dialogue*, paraphrases Buber in writing that "responsibility cannot be laid down according to any set principle but must be ever again recognized in the depths of the soul according to the demands of each concrete situation."[8] Joseph Fletcher also emphasized the need to respond to unique situations rather than abstract principles when he stated , "The situation ethicist says … it is a moral mistake to ask *whether* a thing such as lying is right or wrong universally and in the abstract; that the correct question is *when* it is right and *when* it is wrong."[9]

Our curriculum team struggled mightily with these issues while developing the curriculum and came down firmly on the side of situation ethics. Our own life experience taught us that in all but the most simple situations, attempting to resolve a moral dilemma by arbitrarily applying an abstract principle seldom dealt with the complexity of the situation and even less often resulted in universal agreement about what should be done. We believed that most solutions are limited and not all conflicts can be resolved. We agreed with Dietrich Bonhoeffer's discussion of the "structure of responsibility" in his *Ethics*, where he stated that there is no "absolute good" that is to be realized. On the contrary, the responsible agent prefers what is relatively better to what is relatively worse, and perceives that the "absolute good" may sometimes be the very worst.[10]

Kohlberg was such a dominant figure in the field of moral development that one did not reject his perspective without careful consideration. At some point in the development of the *Decision Making* curriculum, I requested and obtained a meeting with Kohlberg to review and evaluate the materials we were developing. At the time, he was teaching at the University of Chicago. We had a tense lunch at the Faculty Club at the University, but a most cordial extended meeting in his office afterwards, where we agreed to disagree. By the time *Decision Making* was completed and published, Kohlberg had moved to a faculty position at Harvard. We were intrigued to discover that he worked to get himself invited to several UU churches in the Boston area to explain the difference between his point of view and that of our curriculum. We were also intrigued with his book on *The Philosophy of Moral Development*, in which he used some of the learning activities from *Decision Making* to contrast his own point of view with that of situation ethics. We were always pleased when work we were doing in curriculum development at the UUA contributed to the ongoing conversation in the larger world regarding significant philosophical issues.

Ten years later I was fascinated by Carol Gilligan's analysis of Kohlberg's position. The eighty-four subjects on whom Kohlberg based his study were all male. He had followed their development from their childhood years into adulthood. Gilligan did not necessarily reject the possibility that Kohlberg's work is applicable for men. However, she anchored women's decision making at its most mature stage in a conception of responsibility that is Kohlberg's stage-four dilemma for men — "how to lead a moral life which includes obligations to myself, and my family and people in general."[11] Thus, while in Kohlberg's scheme, men at the highest stage worry about interfering with each other's rights, women worry about the possibility of omission, of not helping others when one could have, *and the limitations of any particular resolution along with the unresolved conflicts that remain, which is precisely the position of the situation ethicist.*[12]

Critical Issue: What's Religious?

Another critical issue that had to be resolved as we developed a new curriculum series was: what topics belong in a religious education program? The issue kept arising when parents in some of our local societies asked, "What's religious about some of the curricula being developed, such as *Decision Making, Human Heritage,* and *Man the Culture Builder?* Aren't these secular topics that are rightly a part of the educational offerings in public schools but not in the religious education programs of our churches?"

In my judgment, the questions reflect a lack of awareness of the circumstances in which we live at the turn of the twenty-first century and how the meaning of the term *secular* has changed over time. In the thinking that follows, I acknowledge the influence of one of the major theologians of the 1960s and 1970s, Richard R. Niebuhr, who taught at the Harvard Divinity

School during that period. His little book, *Experiential Religion*, is one of the gems of theological discourse.

Niebuhr points out that the word *secular* used to refer to spheres of life that were perceived as being in opposition to the sacred or religious. Prior to the sixteenth century, for example, the Christian Church was the chief shaper of culture in the Western world. However, beginning in the sixteenth century and continuing into the twentieth, the power and influence of the church declined dramatically and the so-called secular world of commerce and industry took its place. One could say that each generation from Luther to Freud was less profoundly touched by religious institutions, and more and more affected by powerful secular influences in contrast or opposition to them.

Today, our experience of the secular world has changed. For the distinctive element in our lives is not the power of one institution over another, such as the greater authority of banks and the diminished authority of churches. Rather, our experience of the secular world is of the *power* of an *incredible multiplicity* of influences that impinge upon us from all directions, persuading and coercing us, demanding our attention. It is an experience to which we have opened ourselves with the development of communications technology, extending our range of awareness far beyond whatever drummed upon the ears of our ancestors.

We exist in a world that bombards us with the power of these myriad influences — power driving and moving us, distracting and destroying us, healing and shaping us. "It is," as Niebuhr wrote, "at every level an intrusive world, an insistent and abrasive world, in every part capable of opposing our intentions, deflecting us from our courses, thwarting our plans, and transforming our purposes. It is also an extraordinary and miraculous world, filling some moments with delight and astonishment. Again, it can be an agreeable world, yielding to our designs and forms. But it is never an indifferent world."[13] This is our experience of the secular world today. It is not the opposite of the religious. It is much more. The secular is the whole age, laying upon us an obligation to play our part in the building up of a common good.

These are also the circumstances, according to Niebuhr, in which religion arises. He suggested that religion arises from the sense of being aimed at by powers coercive and persuasive, which affect us *totally*: as intellectual beings, as moral beings, as aesthetic beings, as sentient beings, and as biological beings. *"Religion arises as human reaction and answer to the state of being affected totally."*[14] Living in the midst of *powers* that impinge upon us and affect us *totally*, we attempt to *orient* ourselves within this power-filled world. *This perennial striving for orientation is human religiousness. In this need for orientation, religion forms itself.*

One of the influences whose power impinges upon us and shapes us at every moment of our lives is the great drama of biological evolution. Orienting ourselves to the nature and needs of this great life process, in which each of us participates and to which each of us must respond, is one of the tasks of a living religion. This is why a curriculum such as *Human Heritage*, a program whose inclusion in the curriculum was questioned by members of some of our churches and fellowships, should be an integral part of every religious education program for children and young people. Developed by Joan Goodwin, the program had its inception at Meadville/Lombard Theological School with the help of Ralph Burhoe, director of the Center for Advanced Studies in Theology and the Sciences, who understood its importance. It provides children with an experience of how the power of biological evolution affects every moment of their lives and helps to orient them to this influence. It calls upon them to honor it and to incorporate it into their rudimentary faith about the life process. Joan wrote in her introduction to the curriculum:

> Hopefully the awareness will come that each of us began long before a personal day of birth, that our beginning was one with the beginning of life, and that ancient ways of growing and knowing discovered by countless forms of life since that beginning still live in us and shape the lives we call our own ... We must understand the nature and needs of this life process of which we are an expression, and we must heed and honor

them in the way we live our individual lives. The alternative is death—not the creative death which is an integral part of life, but that final death which may end the story of life on the planet Earth.[15]

Orienting children and ourselves to this great drama and helping them become aware of the need to heed and honor the life process is becoming increasingly important. We have assumed a dominion over life of which the priestly liturgists had no inkling. Niebuhr recognized this when he wrote, "Increasingly we have appropriated the prerogative of Darwin's impersonal principle of natural selection and henceforth the direction of our growth depends largely on what *we* shall deem to be natural or right or good for mankind."[16] On one of the days I was working on this section of my presentation, an article appeared in the *International Herald Tribune* titled, "Science Building a Better Mouse."[17] The headline referred to the old-fashioned mouse, the kind that scampers across your basement floor, not the one you use to give directions to your computer. The article stated that scientists had, for the first time, created a strain of mice significantly smarter than normal by adding a simple gene to the rodent's brain. A seemingly minor genetic manipulation improved performance on a wide range of learning and memory tasks. The article further stated that this achievement has brought a sense of immediacy to a long-simmering debate about the ethics of genetic enhancements and making human "designer babies." On a recent TV show, one participant called our growing ability to manipulate genetic structure the atom bomb of our generation.

Another influence whose power impinges upon us and shapes us at every moment of our lives is our expanded and intensified awareness of the heterogeneity we encounter within the human community. The many ways of being human formulated by our neighbors around the world and the authenticity of their experience leaves us in a state of astonishment. If we believe that nothing human is foreign to us, we find the different ways of others to be as worthy of being scrutinized, tested, and honored as the inherited faith of our mothers and fathers. When we do, we often find our own version of humanity challenged and our faith in need of expanding and deepening. We are molded and influenced by many powers and, as Niebuhr suggested, the task for each of us is to find our own humanity and religious orientation in the midst of this diversity without disdain for the materials given us through and by the complexity around us.[18]

Children ages nine to twelve are introduced to a relatively simple instance of this "manyness" through an encounter with the Navajo of the Painted Desert in a curriculum titled *Man the Culture Builder, Part I*, by Walter Bateman. Through a variety of learning activities, the children learn how the ecology of the land impinged upon the Navajo and affected them totally as intellectual, moral, aesthetic, sentient, and biological beings, and influenced and shaped their ways of surviving. They encounter the social organization and kinship systems that the Navajo developed to survive. And they discover, as Niebuhr suggested, how religion arises as human reaction and answer to the state of being affected totally. Believing, for instance, that illness results from having done wrong to some aspect of the ecology, the Navajo faith seeks to restore a person's orientation and harmony with the beauty and mystery and holiness of the natural world. To restore harmony a Singer may offer the Shooting Chant prayer:

> Let me drink the dewdrops again,
> Let me taste the yellow pollen again,
> Let me live in beauty again,
> Let me walk in strength again,
> Make it beautiful wherever I go
> From the top of the red mesas
> To the twilight of the purple evening
> From the blue of the rainbow sky
> To the black darkness of the night
> Make it beautiful wherever I go.[19]

Man the Culture Builder, Part II, also by Bateman, provided similar experiences with a second culture, the !Kung of the Kalahari.

Children ages five to seven have similar experiences of the diversity of the human community, including a variety of religious orientations, through encounters with a remarkable curriculum titled *The Adventures of God's Folk* by Joseph Bassett and Joan Hunt. Using the terms "realms of being" and "forms of being" rather than Niebuhr's "powers," Bassett and Hunt described how each of us lives in various realms of being and encounters a variety of forms of being that shape us as we engage in the many adventures of our lives. Some of the realms of being are identified by the space they occupy, such as the planet earth, large cities and farm areas, apartment complexes or single-family dwellings, lake regions or even deserts. Other realms of being in which we live are identified by the periods of time they encompass. We live, for instance, in the twenty-first century, the nuclear age, and the age of individualism. We also live in realms of being that are the creations of our culture. Thus many of us live in a middle-class society, work in industrial complexes and educational institutions, and live in nuclear or extended families. Forms of being are people and the activities in which they engage. They are also the other living things we encounter as well as the many inanimate objects that fill the realms of being in which we live.[20]

Every day of our living requires responses from each of us to the various realms of being in which we live and the forms of being we meet within them. Because, as with Niebuhr's "powers," they have an effect upon us, each moment of time requires a response of consent to or dissent from one or another of the realms and forms that fill the world we inhabit. How we consent to or dissent from these challenges affects whether we create ways of living in relative harmony with them or whether our lives are a succession of discordant notes.[21]

In *The Adventures of God's Folk* children were introduced through stories to human figures from the Biblical and North American folk traditions. The stories told of the realms and forms the figures encounter in their adventures, the ways in which they consent to and dissent from them, and the religious orient-

ations they evolve. The curriculum praised those people who
consented and dissented with understanding hearts, that is, with
wisdom and empathy. Children were introduced to figures like
Bezalel, Craftsman Extraordinary; David and Solomon in Their
Glorious City; Elijah—Here, There, and Everywhere; Harriet
Tubman, the Beautiful Black Moses; The Pilgrims, Scared and
Befriended; Christmas People in Story and Legend; Sacajawea,
the Remarkable Woman Who Accompanied Lewis and Clark;
Mike Fink, Cockalorum Hero and King of the River; and Johnny
Appleseed, Pioneer of the Wilderness and Sower of Blessings.

Still another curriculum, *Focus on Noah* by Charlene Brotman, offered children a similar experience with the ways Noah
responded to the realms and forms of being he encountered in
his time.

Freedom and Responsibility by Hugo Hollerorth identifies
some of the human qualities that religious liberals have found
essential to achieving a religious orientation in an intrusive
and abrasive but also extraordinary and miraculous world. The
curriculum provides opportunities for junior high young people
to explore the importance of human qualities such as freedom,
responsibility, sensitivity, honesty, love, independence, self-
discipline, self-identity, and adventurousness.

Two other curricula, both by Jane Latourette, also focus on
the qualities and skills we need to live religiously in the world.
Man the Meaning Maker focuses on the fact that although different
people may be exposed to the same external environment, their
perceptions vary in some degree. Even when several people
focus on precisely the same thing, there are still individual
differences in meaning and comprehension. When this happens,
the key question becomes: "How will these differences in
perception be handled?" Do we engage in heated dispute or
in scornful comments, or break off communication and refrain
from further contact? Or do we demonstrate a degree of willing-
ness to continue exchanging and exploring differing views
and meanings? The goal of *Man the Meaning Maker* is to help
participants become more aware of their sensing-responding
selves, more alert to human limitations and the possibilities of

distortion in their perceptions, more ready to expect individual differences in views and meanings, and more willing to accept and make constructive uses of these differences.

Person to Person Communication, also by Latourette, focuses on the importance of language to the human enterprise but also how its imperfections hamper our efforts, as do our abuses and misuses of this distinctive human invention. The curriculum helps young people at the junior high level and older discover the ways that words can be used to manipulate people, the prevalence of divisive name calling, the misperception generated by the frequent use of "is," the unanswerableness of many of our questions, the consequences of overlooking the need for feedback, and other attitudes toward language that make misunderstandings so easy. The ability to use language to communicate more effectively is essential for orienting ourselves to a power-filled world.

Critical Issue: Usability of Materials

A final critical issue with which we had to deal as we began creating programs in the new curriculum series was how to ensure the usability of the materials in a local church or fellowship school. Most of the curriculum kits were created by development teams appointed through the Division of Education and Program office, though in some instances an individual had been working alone or with others on a curriculum in a local society and presented it to the Division office to be considered for publication.

People with various backgrounds and skills were needed for a productive curriculum team. Each team had one or more members who were expert in the subject matter of the program. In the *Man the Culture Builder* series, for example, Ruth Underhill, the renowned anthropologist who had lived among and written about the Navajo, was a major resource person. Skilled educators from the secular field who were also attuned to Unitarian Universalism were sought out as team members. In the culture builder series, Edwin Dethlefsen, the unit director of the Anthropology Curriculum Study Project of the American Anthropological Association, was recruited, along with Robert Spaulding, whom I mentioned earlier. Directors of religious education in our local societies were always major contributors to the development process. Eileen Day from our Germantown church, Caroline Fenderson from our church in Orlando, Kay Hoffman from the Atlanta church, Ellen Massey from the North Shore Unitarian Society in Plandome, New York, and Edna Bruner of the Education Division staff brought the perspective of children's needs and what volunteer lay church school teachers would find useable in our local societies. Walter Bateman, a UU and an intriguing educator who taught anthropology at Rochester Junior College in Rochester, Minnesota, was the writer. Walter's wife, Sue, was our director of religious education in Rochester.

A curriculum team would meet for three to four days at a local church or conference site and begin to conceive the scope of the program and its various parts. After the meeting, the team would take a two- to three-month break, during which time the writer would begin to put the ideas of the team into a curriculum format. The team would then meet for another three or four days, evaluate the work of the writer, approve, disapprove, make suggestions, add to, subtract, deepen, widen—whatever was needed. This process might be repeated three or four times until the team had a product in which it believed and which it wanted to try out in a number of local societies. Of course, while this was going on, first drafts of educational games, filmstrips, card sorts, photographic essays, recordings, puzzles, books, and other teaching aids were being created to use with the learning activities described in the leader's guide.

Most curricula were field tested in fifteen to twenty local societies, usually in a particular UU district or sub-section. Care was taken to include societies of various sizes. Teachers from the field-testing societies would gather for a three-day weekend to be oriented to the curriculum by the team. During the orientation we used the materials with the teachers in the same way we expected the teachers to use them with the children, youth, or adults for whom they were developed. Teachers then returned to their local societies, and for the next half or full year, depending on the length of the curriculum, sent weekly evaluations to the Division of Education office. Sometimes a second weekend meeting was held with the teachers halfway through the testing period, with a final evaluation meeting at the end of the field test. The developmental team used the results of the field test to make revisions in the program, after which it was moved into production and published in a kit form.

At this point, Gene Navias would swing into action and develop a training model to be used to orient groups of teachers from multiple local societies to the new material. Gene, with the help of others, crisscrossed the continent, meeting with groups of teachers from a district for a weekend, at summer conferences, or wherever he could corral them. His idea of developing a training model for each new curriculum was ingenious, in that once some of our directors and advanced teachers experienced it, they were able to use the model themselves to train additional people. After Margaret Odell became a field consultant for the Ohio-Meadville District, she became an invaluable addition to the training process.

Despite the extensive efforts to ensure the usability of the materials, some small church and fellowship schools found it difficult to adapt them to their particular situations. This was especially true for schools that had only enough children enrolled for one class, with the age range of its members extending over five or six years. Adapting the learning activities offered in the curricula in ways that would engage children of such a wide age range proved to be an insurmountable challenge in some schools. The Division of Education and Program attempted to help by publishing supplements to some of the previously pub-lished curricula. Two such publications were *So You Want to Use "Human Heritage" in Your Small Church or Fellowship School* and *So You Want to Use "Man the Culture Builder" in Your Small Church or Fellowship School*. The supplements suggested imaginative ways to use the programs in a small-school setting, often describing ways other schools had adapted them.

Adult Education

The Division of Education and Program had never become involved in any substantial way in the creation of adult education materials. However, the growing interest in adult education in our churches and fellowships as well as in the culture at large during the 1960s and 1970s resulted in suggestions that the Division develop curricula for adults as well as for children and youth. As with the curricula for children and youth, some of the materials that were published were developed in local societies and submitted to the Division to be considered for publication. Other curricula were created by development teams appointed through the Curriculum Development Office.

Project Listening, the first adult curriculum published, evolved through the efforts of Herbert Adams to improve communication between youth and their parents in the Follen Church of Lexington, Massachusetts, where he was the minister. William Rogers of the Harvard Divinity School served as a consultant on the program's development. The program was designed to improve communication by providing basic training in one of the skills most necessary for community — the skill of good listening.

A second program published by the Division, *Employing Your Total Self* by Josiah Bartlett, evolved primarily through the efforts of a single individual rather than a curriculum team. Bartlett, the recently retired dean of the Starr King School for the Ministry in Berkeley, California, had been developing the program for some time as a part of his work: helping people to answer the profoundly religious question, "What do I really want to do with my life?" by clarifying their career/life goals. Participants in the program acquired a vivid awareness of their skills and strengths and how they could be combined and recombined in a variety of clusters to qualify them for diverse paid or volunteer job situations. The program helped people in any stage of their lives to become aware of their possibilities, to shape and reshape their career/life goals, and to build the confidence to implement them.

As suggested in the introduction to this presentation, the 1960s and 1970s were times of upheaval in the larger society and in our own UU community. Such periods of ferment and change evoke questioning, anxiety, and doubt. This time of rapid change raised questions about what gives us our character and identity as Unitarian Universalists. What binds us together? What unites us with our past? Is there a center that holds despite changing religious formulations, evolving dynamics within our religious community, and new strategies for relating to the larger world?

It was no doubt an awareness of these and other troubling questions that prompted Robert West, president of the UUA, to suggest that the Department of Education and Social Concern (a new name for the Division of Education and Program) develop eduational curricula for adults that provided opportunities for clarifying our personal and institutional identity as Unitarian Universalists. He believed that beneath the seething turmoil, we shared perceptions, convictions, and commitments that united us, which needed to be lifted up, recognized, affirmed, and celebrated. In response to this challenge, a development team was appointed, which over a period of five years developed a three-part educational series called "The Way We Are: Exploring Our Unitarian Universalist Identities." Part I was titled *The Disagreements Which Unite Us;* Part II was *Our Experiencing, Believing, and Celebrating,* and Part III was *Our Ways Of Relating.*

David Johnson, at the time our minister in the Unitarian Universalist Church of Tucson, Arizona, was the major author of *The Disagreements Which Unite Us.* Johnson pointed out that the histories of Unitarianism and Universalism are commonly viewed in one of two ways: as a step-by-step refining, over the years, of our central principles and commitments; or as a succession of disagreements over time around substantial issues for which there are no final and absolute answers. Both interpretations, according to Johnson, are true. Our histories do reflect a gradual clarification of our basic principles. However, our histories are also a succession of disagreements – disagreements among persons, over issues, often within the context of conflicts between a new generation and its predecessors.[22]

Sixteen issues – eight from our Unitarian history and eight from our Universalist heritage – provided the focus of Johnson's *Disagreements*. Johnson engaged users of the curriculum in exploring these issues anew. Each issue was at one time the focus of a critical disagreement, a turning point, a fundamental theological and institutional crisis, a time of sifting and sorting. Each issue is also alive today as UUs ponder their theological convictions, determine their societal commitments, and create and live out the dynamics of their religious community. Each issue was explored through encountering and reflecting upon two forceful opposing positions by two major contenders during a period in our history when the issue was of special concern. The list of the contenders was a virtual "Who's Who" of Unitarian and Universalist history. Participants also learned about the historical circumstances that evoked the disagreement and about the lives of the major contenders. Through role playing, debate, and dialogue, participants reflected on how the issue affected their lives together: in their homes, churches, fellowships, and larger communities. The program offered a feast of Unitarian Universalist heritage.

Partway through the development of the curriculum, Johnson proposed to Gene Navias that he assemble a hymnbook containing the words and music to a few of the great profusion of hymns and songs written by Unitarians and Universalists during our two hundred years of history in North America. Gene was particularly interested in hymns written by some of the contenders on various sides of the issues with which Johnson's curriculum dealt. The result was a dazzling collection of hymns titled *Singing Our History*, an enriching supplement to the curriculum and the source of hours of enjoyment as participants in the program sang as well as debated our history.

Part II of the series, *Our Experiencing, Believing, and Celebrating*, provided participants with an experience of the rich, radiant, celebrative commonality and diversity that gives our Unitarian Universalist movement vitality and creativity. One of the more intriguing units of the program was "Unitarian Universalist East-West Identity" by Vern Barnet. The activities of the unit provided participants an opportunity to become more aware of how they experienced and understood the world, as well as the styles they had evolved for relating to it. In particular, they discovered the similarities and differences between their own personal styles of relating and those of Western and Eastern philosophies and modes. What made this an intriguing unit was the discovery that many of our UU congregations had more affinity for the Eastern mode than the Western.

Part III of the series, *Our Ways of Relating,* consisted of units such as "The UU Status Game," which provided participants an opportunity to explore the factors that make for advantages and disadvantages in status among members of UU churches and fellowships. Other units explored issues such as churches and fellowships as caring communities, the roles of women and men in our local societies, pluralism versus homogeneity in our churches and fellowships, and other questions related to how our local societies operate.

Failed Efforts

In the introductory pages of this essay, I mentioned that a struggle erupted within the UU community over how best to support the civil rights movement in the broader culture. The struggle resulted in the 1969 General Assembly granting a form of empowerment to a segment of our black membership known as the Black Unitarian Universalist Caucus (BUUC). Immediately after the General Assembly, the Education Department joined with BUUC in a commitment to develop an educational curriculum on racism for junior high young people. The program was to be called *Black America/White America: Understanding the Discord.* For various reasons the effort did not succeed. A curriculum dealing with a related topic was published in 1976. It was titled *Africa's Past – Impact on Our Present,* by Musa Eubanks. Its objectives included helping non–African Americans to become aware of the rich traditions and immense achievements of the ancestors of African Americans and to value and respect these traditions and achievements as they became a part of American culture.

Another failed effort was the attempt to develop a curriculum on Unitarian Universalism for upper elementary-age children. A curriculum team was appointed but, again for various reasons, the effort did not congeal. A curriculum team brought together to create a major statement of the Unitarian Universalist philosophy of religious education had a similar experience. Subsequent to that effort, Hugo Hollerorth produced a major pamphlet titled *Relating to Our World: The Philosophy of Religious Education Undergirding the Multimedia Curriculum Series of the Unitarian Universalist Association*. It set forth some of the philosophy articulated in this essay but it was not the major statement originally envisioned. The failure of each of these undertakings was a great disappointment, especially to those who had committed effort and time to them.

About Your Sexuality

About Your Sexuality deserves its own special section in this presentation. Shortly after arriving at the UUA in 1965, I began to receive letters from local societies inquiring if the Division of Education had published any sexuality education materials or recommended those of some other agency. These inquiries came from people in some of our local societies, who believed that our children and young people were seeking help with this most important area of their lives. The UUA had not published its own materials, so we began a systematic study of programs available from non-UUA sources. We found adequate materials on topics like anatomy and venereal disease. There were some good resources dealing with conception, childbirth, and birth control. However, many of us knew from our work with young people that it was areas like masturbation, "making out," homosexuality, and lovemaking that were the most puzzling and troublesome to them. Most materials were strangely silent about these very normal expressions of sexuality. The few materials we did find were exceedingly judgmental and negative toward these behaviors in the lives of young people. The attitudes they expressed seemed diametrically opposed to our conviction that sex is a positive and enriching force in life, that some expression of it is normal and to be expected at all age levels, and that there is no one right norm of sexual behavior for all people. Dissatisfied with what we had found, the staff decided to develop its own program with, I must add, very little idea of what we were undertaking.

Elaine Smith was the director of religious education in our Seattle church while she taught in the Division of Home and Family Education at the North Seattle Community College. I do not remember how she happened to know deryck calderwood, but she facilitated his becoming the theme leader at a Fall Conference of the Liberal Religious Education Directors Association (LREDA). At the time, he was associate professor of health education at New York University. The Fall Conference was an unforgettable experience. I remember his arranging us in small circles of approximately eight people. Each of us in our respective circle was to take a turn being the adult leader while the others in the circle were to assume the role of junior high young people. As each person took the leadership role, deryck tossed out a question. The leader was to assume that one of the junior high young people had asked it and had to attempt to answer it for the young people.

I've never forgotten the question which deryck tossed my way when it was my turn to be the leader in my circle. The question was, "You're a junior high boy walking home from school holding your girl's hand and you get a 'hard-on.' What do you do?" In my mind's eye I traveled back thirty years in half an instant to walking up Monroe Street with Jane to the bus stop in Jefferson City, Missouri, holding her hand, getting a hard-on, and agonizing about what to do. I had very little idea about what was going on and nowhere to turn to help me understand. I couldn't talk with my parents. Sex was never mentioned in my home. It was inconceivable to me to talk with someone at my church. I couldn't talk with my peers. They would have laughed all the way to the lot behind the garage, though in retrospect I realize they were probably suffering from similar confusions and puzzlements about sexuality. The only redeeming factor in my situation was that I was a studious kid who always carried an armload of books home each day. They were just the shield I needed to hold in front of my "hard-on" so that no one, especially Jane, would notice any protrusion. In the small circle that day I was able to tell junior high young people that getting a "hard-on" while walking home holding your girl's hand is a very natural thing to happen, a very normal thing, even a very nice thing.

The Fall Conference convinced all of us that deryck calderwood should be recruited to lead our efforts in developing a sexuality curriculum that responded to the needs of young people. Most readers of this essay probably know the result. The UUA created and published a ground-breaking curriculum that evoked the admiration and support of many other religious groups, public and private schools, a variety of human service agencies, colleges and universities, and countless young people and adults who participated in the program in a variety of educational settings.

One controversial part of the program was the explicit visuals. The development team became committed to the visuals for a variety of reasons. We knew that the youth of that period were visually oriented. They had become accustomed to photographic presentations of everything from fetal life to space exploration. Visual aids had become an integral part of the formal educational process in almost every conceivable subject. It seemed obvious that the omission of explicit sexual visuals in our program would reinforce the concept of sex as something dirty, sinful, and forbidden. John Rich, an authority at that time in child psychiatry,[23] supported this view, as did Dr. John Money of the Pediatric Department at Johns Hopkins.[24] SIECUS, the prestigious sex education organization, took no official position. However, since deryck calderwood was on the SIECUS board, we knew their members represented various persuasions. Initially the visuals consisted of "arty" black-and-white photographs. They were aesthetically pleasing, although much of what was happening was concealed in shadow and obviously staged positions. During the field test, the young people objected to the photographs, maintaining they were of little assistance in helping them visualize what went on during various sexual behaviors. We decided to develop our own visuals, which were used in a second field test and received enthusiastically by most of the young people and their adult leaders.

The program had a vigorous opponent: the district attorney in Brookfield, Wisconsin. The course had been published and we were busily preparing teachers in local societies to use it. Our Brookfield church was one of these societies. A member of the church who was a feature story writer for the *Milwaukee Journal* wrote an appreciative account of the program for the *Journal*. Brookfield was located was in an extromely conservative Catholic diocese. The John Birch Society was active in the area. The *Journal* article came to the attention of the ambitious district attorney, who was looking ahead to his next election campaign. Based on the article, which mentioned the explicit visuals, the district attorney decided the program might be in violation of the obscenity statutes of the State of Wisconsin. He asked the Brookfield church for permission to review the filmstrips before they used the program. The church perceived the district attorney's actions as an effort at censorship and courageously refused him access to the material. He then threatened to ask a state court for an injunction against the church's use of the program until he had evaluated it. The Brookfield church turned to the UUA.

There were giants on the earth in those days and one of them was Frank Frederick, general counsel for the UUA. Frank was the prototype of a Brahmin Yankee — tall, dignified, white hair, a face that displayed the wisdom of his sixty-plus years. Frank immediately took his stand and vowed to preserve the right of the UUA to determine the content of its religious education programs. Robert West, by this time the president of the UUA, was also a giant. Against the counsel of some of his staff who believed that *About Your Sexuality* would be extremely divisive in the

Association, he carefully evaluated the program and supported its publication. Other giants were the Brookfield church and certainly the UUA itself.

Frederick contacted the law firm of Greenbaum, Wolfe and Ernst in New York City. While primarily a huge corporate law firm, one corner of its operation was run by two women attorneys who for years had specialized in obscenity cases. They had successfully defended the publication of literary classics such as *Lady Chatterley's Lover* and *Portnoy's Complaint.* Believing that obscenity cases were more difficult to win in state than federal courts, they recommended that the UUA petition the Federal District Court in Milwaukee for an injunction against the district attorney interfering in the affairs of the Brookfield church. As representation in Milwaukee by two New York lawyers might prejudice the case, they recruited a young UU couple, both attorneys, from one of our Midwest churches to represent the Brookfield church and the UUA. I flew to Milwaukee with one of the New York lawyers, where she gave the young lawyers a crash course in obscenity law.

A petition for an injunction against the district attorney was filed and granted by the Federal District Court in Milwaukee. The district attorney responded by filing an appeal in a three-judge Federal Appeals Court in Chicago. The Appeals Court upheld the injunction, which prompted the DA to file an appeal with the United States Supreme Court in Washington, D.C.

Since one of the three judges in Chicago had been out of the country at the time of the hearing, the Supreme Court justices returned the case to the Appeals Court with the directive that it be ruled on a second time with all three judges present. The justices also stipulated that if the case were referred back to them a second time, they would uphold the original injunction of the District Court in Milwaukee. In the meantime, the district attorney ran for reelection and was defeated by a marvelous coalition of liberals who supported the program and conservatives who were angry that so much tax money was being spent in pursuing the religious education program of a local church. A new district attorney was elected, and he ceased any further action against the Brookfield church.

The UUA also published a three-part audio-visual program called *The Invisible Minority — The Homosexuals in Our Society*. The program won the Annual Award of the National Council of Family Relations as the best audio-visual educational program. The announcement of the award coincided with a tension-filled meeting of the UUA Board of Trustees over whether or not to fund a Gay/Lesbian Affairs Office at the UUA. To deepen the discussion being carried on by the trustees, I was asked to provide an opportunity for them to view the program. I still remember a stress-filled evening in a darkened suite at the old Statler Hilton Hotel in Boston as some twenty-five trustees and denominational officials sat through a good part of the evening viewing the program.

I would like to conclude by making a brief reference to almost everyone's favorite curriculum, *The Haunting House*. It stands as a model of what the developers of the multi-media curriculum series were attempting to create. Its strengths are many, and it shares them with the other curricula of the series. It is experientially grounded in the world of children. It provides children with a rich environment to explore ,and it trusts their capacities to grow or intuit their own understandings over time. It is solidly grounded philosophically, in this case in the work of the French philosopher Gaston Bachelard, as well as in Barbara Hollerorth's rich background of literature and human experience. Its central thrust is to provide children opportunities to orient themselves to the boundlessness and complexity of the power-filled world. The care with which it was field tested in our local societies prior to publication has made it useable in a great variety of church and fellowship settings.

It was a glorious privilege to serve as director of curriculum development at the UUA and I was especially blessed that my opportunity to do so came in the 1960s and 1970s. It was an era of adventure, imagination, risk-taking, and questioning, with which I and others who worked on the curricula had an affinity. Some of those with whom I worked are here this weekend. I thank them, and many others in absentia, once more for their efforts, and hold dear my memories of working with them.

NOTES

1 Arthur Marwick, *The Sixties* (New York: Oxford University Press, 1998), 3.

2 Fund-raising letter for Friends of the UUA from John Buehrens, President of the UUA, May 1999.

3 Clyde Dodder and Barbara Dodder, *Decision Making* (Boston: Beacon Press, 1968), 3-6.

4 Dodder and Dodder, *Decision Making*, 63-64.

5 *The Free Church in a Changing World* (Boston: UUA, 1963), 58.

6 A reference to the title of Angus MacLean's pamphlet, *The Method Is the Message* (Boston: Division of Education and Program, UUA, 1962).

7 Lawrence Kohlberg, *The Philosophy of Moral Development*, vol. 1 (San Francisco: Harper and Row, 1981), 167.

8 Maurice Friedman, *Martin Buber: The Life of Dialogue* (Chicago: University of Chicago Press, 1976), 145.

9 Joseph Fletcher, *Moral Responsibility* (Philadelphia: Westminster Press, 1966), 232-33.

10 Dietrich Bonhoeffer, *Ethics* (Minneapolis: Fortress Press, 2005), 261.

11 Carol Gilligan, *In a Different Voice: Psychological Theory and Women's Development* (Cambridge: Harvard University Press, 1982), 21.

12 Gilligan, *In a Different Voice*, 21-22.

13 Richard Niebuhr, *Experiential Religion* (New York: Harper and Row, 1973), 34.

14 Niebuhr, *Experiential Religion*, 34.

15 Joan Goodwin, *Human Heritage*, Part I (Boston: Beacon Press, 1971), 1.

16 Niebuhr, *Experiential Religion*, 2.

17 "Science Building a Better Mouse," *International Herald Tribune*, September 2, 1999, 1.

18 Niebuhr, *Experiential Religion*, 24.

19 Walter Bateman, *The Navajo of the Painted Desert* (Boston: Beacon Press, 1970), 93. The translation of the "Shooting Chant Prayer" is from Gladys

Reichard, *Spider Woman: A Story of Navajo Weavers and Chanters* (1934; reprint, University of New Mexico Press, 1997).

[20] Joseph Bassett and Joan Hunt, *The Adventures of God's Folk* (Boston: UUA, 1978), 3.

[21] Bassett and Hunt, *Adventures of God's Folk*, 3.

[22] David Johnson, *The Disagreements Which Unite Us* (Boston: UUA, 1975), 5.

[23] John Rich, *Catching Up with Our Children: New Perspectives in Sex Instruction* (Toronto: McClelland and Stewart, 1968), 53.

[24] John Money, *The Positive and Constructive Approach to Pornography in General Sex Education, in the Home, and in Sexological Counseling*, Technical Reports of the Commission on Obscenity and Pornography, vol. 4 (Washington, DC: U.S. Government Printing Office, 1970), 345.

BIBLIOGRAPHY

Adams, Herbert and William Rogers. *Project Listening*. Boston. UUA, 1974.

Barnett, Vern, Madlyn Evans, Caroline Fenderson, Hugo Hollerorth, David Johnson, Richard Kellaway, Tom Mikelson, Ellen Nelson, and Robert Tapp. *Our Experiencing, Believing, and Celebrating*. Boston: UUA, 1979.

———. *Our Ways of Relating*. Boston: UUA, 1979.

Bartlett, Josiah. *Employing Your Total Self*. Boston: UUA, 1976.

Bassett, Joseph and Joan Hunt, *The Adventures of God's Folk*. Boston: UUA, 1978.

Bateman, Walter. *Man the Culture Builder, Parts I and II*. Boston: Beacon Press, 1970.

———. *The Navajo of the Painted Desert*. Boston: Beacon Press, 1970.

———. *So You Want to Use "Man the Culture Builder" in Your Small Church or Fellowship School*. Boston: UUA, 1974.

Brotman, Charlene. *Focus on Noah*. Boston: UUA, 1976.

calderwood, deryck. *About Your Sexuality*. Boston: Beacon Press, 1971.

calderwood, deryck and Wasyl Szkodzinsky. *The Invisible Minority — The Homosexuals in Our Society*. Boston: UUA, 1972.

Dodder, Clyde and Barbara Dodder, *Decision Making*. Boston: Beacon Press, 1968.

Eubanks, Musa. *Africa's Past — Impact on Our Present*. Boston: UUA, 1976.

Goodwin, Joan. *Human Heritage, Parts I and II*. Boston: Beacon Press, 1971.

———. *So You Want to Use "Human Heritage" in Your Small Church or Fellowship School*. Boston: UUA, 1973.

Hollerorth, Barbara. *The Haunting House*. Boston: UUA, 1974.

Hollerorth, Hugo. *Freedom and Responsibility*. Boston: Beacon Press, 1969.

———. *Relating to Our World: The Philosophy of Religious Education Undergirding the Multimedia Curriculum Series of the Unitarian Universalist Association*. Boston: UUA, 1974.

Johnson, David. *The Disagreements Which Unite Us*. Boston: UUA, 1975.

Latourette, Jane. *Man the Meaning Maker*. Boston: Beacon Press, 1971.

———. *Person to Person Communication*. Boston: UUA, 1972.

Navias, Eugene B. *Singing Our History: Tales, Texts, and Tunes from Two Centuries of Unitarian and Universalist Hymns*. Boston: UUA, 1975.

M. *Elizabeth Anastos*

THE RE FUTURES ERA
1980-1999

The Unitarians and the Universalists both approached and diverged from mainstream Protestant religious education philosophy and practice during the past two centuries. Divergence was the stronger trend, however; and the movement was always toward more liberal positions in theology, educational philosophy, and psychology, especially developmental psychology, as it became an accepted science and part of the mainstream in the field of education. Each of these was present in the development of Unitarian Universalist religious education in the twentieth century.

In the 1950s and 1960s, religious education played a major role in the growth of congregations, attracting many new families. The educational philosophy and resources developed by Sophia Lyon Fahs, Angus MacLean, Dorothy Spoerl, and Hugo Hollerorth met the challenges and demands of those times and served us well. In the late 1970s, however, new concerns about religious education emerged. Many religious professionals and congregations thought the UUA was not putting sufficient resources into education. Severe financial constraints had ended a concerted effort to produce a steady stream of innovative, quality programs. By 1980, after the resignation of the curriculum editor, Hugo Hollerorth, and with the impending retirement of Jean Starr Williams as director of the Education Section, a major effort was again required to meet the needs of our congregations.

At that time, many Unitarian Universalists were expressing a desire to learn about and develop an identity with Unitarian Universalist values, beliefs, history, and traditions, and to explore their own spirituality within a Unitarian Universalist community. Congregations were struggling with concerns for the elderly, problems stemming from divorce, the availability of drugs, and the increase in violence and crime. Faced with changing societal norms, new research in human development and social sciences, a new emphasis on adult learning, and the increasing impact of technology, the UUA was compelled to re-evaluate its philosophy, materials, and methods in religious education in order to continue to nurture denominational and individual growth.

There was also concern about the level of preparation in religious education being provided for our professional leaders at the graduate level. Our theological schools at St. Lawrence and Tufts Universities, which had strong programs in religious education, closed in the 1960s, and Meadville/Lombard Theological School terminated its short-lived Ministry of Religious Education degree program in 1971.

All of these factors influenced the UUA Board of Trustees, in January 1980, to approve President Eugene Pickett's proposal to appoint a special committee of persons trained and knowledgeable in education and Unitarian Universalism, who could assess the goals and directions congregations were seeking in religious education. The Board and administration acted quickly, and a "blue ribbon" committee was selected in February. I am sure that Eugene Pickett knew well before that January meeting that the Board would approve the proposal, since, in consultation with others, he had already recruited the potential candidates. He had called me in November 1979 and asked me if I would be interested in applying for the position of staff consultant to the committee. I was and I did.

The Committee was charged to assess what was needed in religious education at all levels, from birth to death; to seek out available resources within the movement and beyond; to examine present curriculum resources and determine future needs in terms of staff, materials, and budget; to explore the philosophical grounds of Unitarian Universalist religious education; and to write a comprehensive report of its process, findings, conclusions, and recommendations.

The members of the Religious Education Futures Committee had been carefully selected. Although they represented diverse backgrounds in philosophy, theology, and education, they all had a strong commitment to Unitarian Universalism. The group was enthusiastic about its charge and committed to bringing forth goals and objectives that were appropriate, achievable, and of maximum benefit to the Association. Linda Peebles, in her paper about the Futures Committee's impact, wrote that "Tom Owen-Towle ... believes that what made the experience meaningful was its clear primary emphasis on being a 'think tank' and having the time, energy, focus, and mission to review, assess, and set goals. The process was needed at that time, and made clear contributions to the whole Unitarian Universalist movement."[1]

The Committee's chair, Christine Wetzel, was a skilled facilitator who moved the process along, allowed time for working through disagreements, and encouraged the Committee. The other ministers on the Committee were Judith Hoehler, Clark Olsen, Tom Owen-Towle, and Marshall Grigsby. (Grigsby was assistant dean at Howard University's Theological School in the District of Columbia and president of Benedict College in Columbia, South Carolina.) The lay members were Ann Howe, professor of education at Syracuse University; Nell McGlothlin, educator and member of the UUA Board of Trustees; and Barbara Beach, writer and editor for journals on education and the arts.

We began our task on April 30, 1980. Our report to the Board of Trustees was due in October 1981. The Committee planned and executed a comprehensive process of research, including surveys, interviews, hearings and workshops at General Assembly, and articles in the *UU World* soliciting opinions and recommendations. This resulted in nine working papers by Committee members and myself.

It was fascinating to observe the group dynamics of the Committee as deliberations progressed. Our working relationship was very stimulating, though not always comfortable. Members came with different agendas and deeply held opinions about what the UUA could and should do to develop a strong, multifaceted religious education program, as well as different ideas about the philosophy on which it should rest. We had many disagreements, some passionately argued and defended.

One of the biggest issues we wrestled with was whether to recommend a unified core curriculum (one curriculum for each grade level, preschool through high school), which could be updated as time went on. However, as we listened to congregations, groups, and individuals across the continent, it became apparent that, given the diversity of Unitarian Universalist congregations, a core curriculum could not meet their needs.

Near the end of our deliberations, when a member proposed that we present a majority and a minority report, we discussed the idea fully and then decisively voted it down. In the end, the Committee arrived at unanimous decisions on each section of its final report.

The Committee's Recommendations

Although curriculum and program development was an important and substantive part of the Committee's recommendations, it was only one piece of a broad plan for Unitarian Universalist religious education. Also included were:

- *An Advisory Committee* to the Education Department, appointed by and responsible to the UUA president. Its responsibilities included advising on priorities for the development of curricula, programs, and services, and helping the staff to set goals and to develop evaluation, feedback, and support systems. Unfortunately the committee was discontinued six years later, mostly due to budget cuts.

- *Leadership Development.* The Committee recommended that the Renaissance Program for lay religious educators, as proposed by the Committee on Lay Religious Education Leadership, be implemented by the UUA. Started in 1982 with six training modules, the program has proved extremely successful. The Independent Study Program, to help prepare ministers of religious education, was established by the UUA Board in 1977. Originally administered by the UUA, it was transferred to Meadville/Lombard Theological School in 1992. Following accreditation, in 1993 it became the Modified Residency Program, a degree-granting program at Meadville/Lombard. The UUA's Ministerial Fellowship Committee added religious education preparation to their requirements for parish ministry candidates.

- A *Center for Religious Education* at one of our theological schools, as envisioned by Sophia Fahs. The Sophia Lyon Fahs Center at Meadville/Lombard was dedicated in January 1993.

- *Youth Programs.* The committee urged the UUA to fully support the recommendations of the 1981 Common Ground Youth Assembly to strengthen leadership and resources for youth programs. Work to implement these recommendations had already begun under the guidance of the Youth Program Director, Wayne Arnason, by the time the report was published.

- *Worship.* The Committee recommended that the Ministry and Education Departments cooperate to provide congregations with program resources and professional leadership for worship for all ages. Religious educator Jacqui James joined the Ministry Department to oversee the development of the new hymnal, and later moved to the Religious Education Department as worship resources and diversity coordinator.

- *UUA Staff Positions.* The Committee recommended an increase in staff to carry out the expanded programs, including two full-time regional consultants. As of 1999, we have nine district RE consultants, four of whom are full-time.

The first staff positions to be filled were: Education Director, Eugene Navias; Curriculum Coordinators, David Marshak (a PhD candidate at the Harvard Graduate School of Education) and myself; Director of Children's Programs and REACH Editor, Ann Fields; Dean of the Independent Study Program for Ministry of Religious Education, Judy Mannheim. Youth Programs Director, Wayne Arnason, continued with the transition of LRY (Liberal Religious Youth) to YRUU (Young Religious Unitarian Universalists). In 1985, Judith Frediani joined the Curriculum Office as Curriculum Manager.

• *Continuation of Present Programs.* The group recommended continuing two existing programs: the REACH Packet, a rich potpourri of resources for lifespan religious education leaders; and training workshops to demonstrate the philosophy, content, and method of new and revised curricula to lay leaders.

The Curriculum Model

The Futures Report recommended a three-dimensional model for curriculum development. The dimensions are: 1) the principles of Unitarian Universalism; 2) the resources from which the materials will be drawn; and 3) the developmental levels of the learners.[2]

This was a proposal for both a new curriculum design and a new way of thinking about curriculum development — to unify our efforts while simultaneously affirming our diversity. It took into account different learning abilities and styles, and offered evolving educational opportunities across the lifespan. The UU Principles were to be addressed at each developmental level and illustrated through a variety of source materials.

The Report described the second dimension of the Curriculum Model as:

the primary resources from which illustrations of the principles in action will be drawn. The resource areas are not topics to be taught but will be the source of materials to be used in teaching

the principles of Unitarian Universalism. The resources are:
1. Unitarian Universalist History and Traditions
2. Judeo-Christian Heritage
3. Other World Religions and Cultures
4. The Arts
5. Secular Literature
6. Contemporary and Historical Events and Forces.[3]

The Committee's goal for the religious education program was:

> to assist persons to become men and women who identify and articulate the principles they hold in common, who know the sources of their beliefs, who understand how these principles have been expressed in the lives of people of the past, and who, while aware of the dilemmas and conflicts that their principles may cause today, nonetheless freely choose to act according to those principles.[4]

The Committee reviewed literature on research into moral and faith development, such as that of Lawrence Kohlberg, James Fowler, Robert Kegan and Sharon Daloz Parks. In light of these studies the Committee reported:

> The third element in the Curriculum Model is the developmental level of the learner. During the past two or three decades there have been notable advances in our knowledge of how individuals come to understand important ideas and concepts. More recently this work has been extended to include moral development and faith development not only in childhood and adolescence but throughout the lifespan. It is now the prevailing view that learning depends in large part on the developmental level of the learner, i.e., what a person can learn is both limited and enhanced by his or her level of mental development. The Curriculum Model recognizes the need to take the learner's developmental level into account in all curriculum planning, whether learners are grouped by age level or are taught in multi-age groupings.[5]

New curricula were to be designed "in spiral rather than in linear terms. This means reintroducing the values, concepts, and functional principles of the faith that we affirm at each developmental level of understanding."[6] That, of course, was not new in the 1980s; it was part of James Gallagher's philosophy and had been incorporated into curriculum programs in Hugo Hollerorth's era. The Futures Committee also recommended that we continue to use curriculum teams to create programs, and that each team include persons with knowledge and expertise in the primary resources.

In addition, the Committee recommended evaluating current curricula, incorporating them into the new design wherever feasible, and encouraging the creativity of local congregations and individuals in developing curriculum materials. Rich additions to UU curricula have been made by Mary Ann Moore, Betty Jo Middleton, Barbara A. Marshman, Ann Fields, Charlene Brotman, Margaret Gooding, Virginia Steel, Jane McKeel, Judy Fisher, and Cheryl Binkley, to name but a few.

Philosophy of UU Religious Education

One of the charges of the Futures Committee was to explore the philosophical grounds that would give direction to our programs. At our meeting in May 1981, with research and opinion-gathering completed and agreement reached on several difficult issues, the Committee debated the philosophical grounds on which our recommendations were based. We struggled to articulate a statement that recognizes the theological pluralism among us and yet provides a cohesive framework, highlighting commonly accepted UU principles, within which curricula can be developed. After intensive discussion, the Committee decided to defer further consideration until the next day. The next morning a fruitful discussion led to a cohesive draft statement of the philosophical grounds of Unitarian Universalist religious education. We had captured the core of what we had been examining for several months.

The statement began, "As education is a process of becoming, religious education is a process which nurtures religious becoming. 'Religious growth' and 'faith development' are terms which describe the end-in-view of the religious education process."[7]

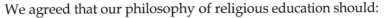

We agreed that our philosophy of religious education should:

- emphasize the total religious community as a learning community
- respect the theological pluralism among us
- embody the UU Principles in stories, art, myths, symbols, and celebrations so that children, youth, and adults can articulate and act upon them
- incorporate insights from contemporary scholarship in developmental psychology, religious studies, and pedagogy
- emphasize a holistic approach, which addresses the whole person — the intellectual, emotional, physical, aesthetic, moral, spiritual, imaginative, and historical-social dimensions of an individual living within an interdependent ecosystem.

The Futures Committee recommended developing and publishing materials that would guide congregations through the process of formulating and articulating a philosophy of religious education. David Marshak and I collaborated on *Philosophy-Making: A Process Guide for Unitarian Universalist Religious Growth and Learning* (1984).

Beginnings

The first programs to emerge in this era were those that had been sent to the RE Department by individual authors or that we had heard about. In 1978, Jean Starr Williams, then director of the RE Department, learned of the preschool program Corelyn Senn had written for her church in Charlottesville, Virginia. Margaret Gooding was recruited as editor to work with Corelyn. *Growing Times* (1980) was the last preschool program published by the UUA until the publication of *Rainbow Children, Celebrating Me and My World, We Are Many, We Are One,* and *Chalice Children* in the late 1990s.

In 1982, we revised Richard Gilbert's *Building Your Own Theology,* publishing that and his *Building Your Own Theology II* in 1983. David Marshak worked with Caroline Fenderson to rewrite, edit, and publish her junior high program, *Life Journey*

(1988). *Life Issues for Teenagers,* by Wayne Arnason and Cheryl Powers, also edited by David Marshak, came out in 1985.

I undertook editing the fourth revised edition of *About Your Sexuality* after Hugo Hollerorth finished the revisions he and deryck calderwood had begun. Sadly, deryck died before the project was completed. The revised edition was published in 1983. I then began working with Shirley Ranck to finish *Cakes for the Queen of Heaven,* an adult curriculum for women, which she had begun in 1978. It was published in 1986 and became a very popular adult program.

Frank Robertson, then Minister of Religious Education at All Souls Unitarian Church in Washington, D.C., submitted *World Religions,* a program for junior high which he had written. David Marshak and Frank Robertson formed a team in the Greater Washington area to continue development of the program. The resulting curriculum was published in 1987. This was the last curriculum kit published by the UUA.

The New Curriculum Teams

In 1985, David and I formed, and began working with, curriculum teams on Peace and Social Justice, Unitarian Universalism, Heritages from Judaism and Christianity, Gender Identity, Spirituality, and Racial Justice. We deliberately formed teams located in different geographical regions of the continent, seeking persons with the skills and knowledge needed for a particular curriculum, to keep from being all Boston-based and to save travel costs.

The Racial Justice team has published two curricula to date: *Rainbow Children,* for ages five to eight, by Norma Poinsett and Virginia Burns; and *Race to Justice,* for junior high, by Robin Gray and José Ballester y Marquez.

The Peace and Social Justice Team

The Peace and Social Justice team, guided by David Marshak, was one of the most successful. Members included Barry Andrews and Patricia Hoertdoerfer. All except Patricia were located in the Pacific Northwest. The team produced the *In Our Hands* programs, for five age levels from grade one through adult. The work was done between 1983 and 1988, with final publication in 1990. Seven years to produce a set of curricula may seem long, but the process covered conceptualizing, writing, rewriting, editing, field testing, more editing, production, and delivery.

The Unitarian Universalism Team

The Unitarian Universalism Team, located in the St. Lawrence District (New York and Ontario), also produced curricula for people of all ages. These included Jan Evans-Tiller's *Around the Church, Around the Year* for primary age students, and two adult curricula: *How Open the Door: The Afro-American Experience in Unitarian Universalism* by Mark Morrison-Reed, and *Our Unitarian Universalist Story* by Carol Meyer (originally begun by Nancy Osborn). In between were Margaret Gooding's *A Stepping-Stone Year*, Lois Ecklund's *Travel in Time*, and Elizabeth Strong's *Messages in Music* — six programs!

These curricula followed a spiral model that gradually informed UUs at each age level about our UU heritage in Europe and North America by tracing our values, beliefs, ethics, and theological stances from the eighteenth century to the present. These curricula showed how Unitarian Universalism has developed from biblical theistic Christianity to humanism and beyond, and broadened to include UU Jews, pagans, Buddhists, mystic humanists, and others.

The Heritages from Judaism and Christianity Team

It is not easy to develop programs on Jewish and Christian history for UUs, even when many congregations are asking for them. Each congregation has a different opinion as to what should be presented and how. Even our Christian UU congregations vary in their choices of curricula for children, for there is a broad theological spectrum among the member congregations of the

Convocation of Christian Churches Within the UUA. Some identify themselves closely with the UUA; others do not. Some use curricula from other denominations in addition to our own. Others have written their own programs, incorporating Unitarian Universalist history, the UU Principles, local church history, etc. Some of the Boston-area churches asked the UUA to publish biblical and Christian history programs specially designed for their congregations. We would have liked to do so, but the numbers of those congregations were so small that it was not financially feasible.

The Heritages team deliberated for almost a year before creating *Timeless Themes: Stories from the Hebrew and Christian Bibles*, a curriculum for third and fourth grades by Nannene Gowdy, Mary Ann Moore, and Marjorie Skwire. The curriculum emerged from a design originally created by Nannene Gowdy and a teacher at the South Nassau Unitarian Church in Freeport, New York. Eugene Navias created an accompanying songbook, *Bible Songs on Timeless Themes*. Choir director Alfa Radford prepared a teaching tape, containing all 35 songs from the songbook, performed by the children's and youth choirs of the Unitarian Universalist church in Belmont, Massachusetts. They were superb! I loved sitting in on the rehearsals and the final recording sessions.

The Heritages team also produced the adult curriculum *Conversations with the Bible* by Stephen Washburn. *Special Times: Honoring Our Jewish and Christian Heritages*, for children in grades 1 and 2, was first conceived by Mary Ann Moore and written by Betty Jo Middleton. Robert Miller wrote a program for adults, *Great Moments in the History of the Christian Church*, which was field tested but never published.

We were frequently asked to commission a new version of *The Church Across the Street*, the classic 1947 curriculum by Reginald Manwell and Sophia Fahs. The new program, *Neighboring Faiths*, which included faith groups beyond the Jewish and Christian traditions, was created by Christine Reed and Patricia Hoertdoerfer. I was happy to see it published in 1997.

Since my retirement in 1992, Judith Frediani has served as Director of Curriculum Development. Many new curricula and other resources have been developed, particularly adult curricula such as the *"Parents As..."* series by Roberta and Christopher Nelson; the *Building Your Own Theology* series by Richard Gilbert; *Life Tapestry* by Jeanne Nieuwejaar, Marcia Bowen, and Richard Stower; *Faithful Choices* by Wayne Arnason; and the Lifespan Series by numerous authors. While I cannot cover all the programs that have been developed since 1981, I wish to recognize the contributions of all the authors who put their hearts and energies into creating them.

Final Remarks

My responsibility at the UUA was to develop curriculum resources that would enable Unitarian Universalist congregations to stimulate, affect, and enhance the religious growth and faith development of children, youth, and adults. But curricula are more than courses of study. Religious education, if we do it well, is a means for developing faith, our own and others'. It provides opportunities for finding meaning in life and meaning in the universe, and for discovering what we stand for, what we live and die for. It helps us express our greatest loves and our deepest loyalties.

Religious education embraces the totality of experience in congregational life: worship, social life, learning, social responsibility, personal support, and fun! It begins the moment we walk onto the grounds and into the building: the encounters in the halls and meeting rooms, in the worship experience, in adult study groups, at potluck suppers, fairs, and committee meetings. It extends beyond the building in social action and service to the larger community. As the RE Futures Report says, "Each group setting, each worship service, each encounter between person and person, is potentially an occasion for what Henry Nelson Weiman called 'creative interchange' — what Martin Buber spoke of as 'the I-Thou relationship' and Paul Tillich spoke of as 'being grasped by ultimate concern.'"[8]

I had this kind of encounter with a group of preschoolers at the Cedar Lane Church in Bethesda, Maryland, shortly before I left it to go to the UUA. The teachers of the four- and five-year-olds were at odds with each other about whether to mention God and how to approach the topic if they did. One thought that simple prayers and graces addressed to God were appropriate in a religious education class; the other felt that such language was not appropriate in a Unitarian Universalist church with its diverse community of believers and nonbelievers. This teacher also felt that children this age were not ready to deal with the abstract concept of God. The teachers asked me to visit the class and to introduce the subject of God in a way that I thought was appropriate.

So I joined the children one Sunday at Circle Time and began our conversation by saying that I had come to talk about something important, that there was a special word for it, *worship*, and that worship meant thinking about things of worth—important things. In worshipping, we think about important questions and possible answers. To stimulate their thinking, I suggested that some big questions were about very big ideas, such as "How did the world begin?" and that other big questions were about smaller things, such as …

Melissa piped up and said, "Oh, I know, like where do my feelings come from? Why do I laugh? Why do I cry? Why aren't I just plain?" — all said with appropriate facial expressions. I acknowledged that these were, indeed, very big questions. Other questions began to pour forth from the children:

"Do only people have feelings? My dog cries."

"When it rains, is the sky crying?"

"Where does the rain go when it goes into the ground?"

"What makes thunder and lightning? They scare me!"

Jason responded, "It's the electricity in the air."

"Oh," said Gregory, who was sitting beside me. "In a book my Daddy read to me, it said the ancient Greeks thought that thunder was the wrath of an angry God."

We were into our subject!

"God is love," responded Amanda, "so God wouldn't be angry and make thunder to scare us."

"God made the world," said Kimberley, "the sky, the trees, the people, everything!"

"Oh yes," said Gregory, knowingly, "You mean the Creator."

"But no one knows if that is really so," rejoined Melissa. "I wonder if people will ever know if it's really so?"

"Yes, we will," said Colin confidently, "'cause we have brains, and brains can think!"

The conversation went on, with all of the children absorbed in the subject. We did not come to any group resolution as to who or what God is. It was not necessary. Every child had his or her own conception of God, whether drawn from parents, friends, or other sources, and all were eager to talk about it.

This was a "creative interchange" among four- and five-year-olds who were "grasped by an ultimate concern." It was an appropriate interchange for a church school classroom. For this was a safe place in which to be challenged by a diverse but affirming community.

A curriculum at work!

NOTES

[1] Linda Olsen Peebles, "The Futures Report — Toward a Ministry of Religious Education: A Paradigm Shift in Unitarian Universalist Education," in *Unitarian Universalism Selected Essays, 1999* (Boston: Unitarian Universalist Ministers' Association, 1999), 24.

[2] Religious Education Futures Committee, *Report of the Religious Education Futures Committee to the Unitarian Universalist Association Board of Trustees* (Boston: UUA, 1981), 11.

[3] *Report of the Religious Education Futures Committee*, 12.

[4] *Report of the Religious Education Futures Committee*, 12.

[5] *Report of the Religious Education Futures Committee*, 14.

[6] *Report of the Religious Education Futures Committee*, 7.

[7] *Report of the Religious Education Futures Committee*, 8.

[8] *Report of the Religious Education Futures Committee*, 8.

BIBLIOGRAPHY

Anastos, Elizabeth and David Marshak. *Philosophy-Making: A Process Guide for Unitarian Universalist Growth and Learning*. Boston: UUA, 1984.

Andrews, Barry, Robert C. Branch, Virginia Lane, and Harold Rosen. *In Our Hands: A Peace and Social Justice Program, Junior High*. Boston: UUA, 1990.

Andrews, Barry and Patricia Hoertdoerfer. *In Our Hands: A Peace and Social Justice Program, Grades 4-6*. Boston: UUA, 1990.

Arnason, Wayne. *Faithful Choices: An Adult Program in Clinical Ethics and Religious Values*. Boston: UUA, 1998.

Arnason, Wayne and Cheryl Powers. *Life Issues for Teenagers* (LIFT). Boston: UUA, 1985.

Ballester y Marquez, José and Robin Gray. *Race to Justice*. Boston: UUA, 1995.

Bowen, Marcia, Jeanne Nieuwejaar, and Richard Stower. *Life Tapestry*. Boston: UUA, 1994.

Branch, Robert C. , Samuel Goldenberg, and Mary Thomson. *In Our Hands: A Peace and Social Justice Program, Adults*. Boston: UUA, 1990.

calderwood, deryck. *About Your Sexuality* (Revised Edition). Boston: UUA, 1983.

Ecklund, Lois E. *Travel in Time: Unitarian Universalism for Grades 5 and 6*. Boston: UUA, 1989.

Erslev, Kate Tweedie. *Chalice Children: A Unitarian Universalist Preschool Curriculum*. Boston: UUA, 1998.

Evans-Tiller, Jan. *Around the Church, Around the Year: Unitarian Universalism for Children, Kindergarten through Grade 2*. Boston: UUA, 1990.

Fenderson, Caroline. *Life Journey*. Boston: UUA, 1988.

Gilbert, Richard S. *Building Your Own Theology: Volume 1 and 2*. Boston: UUA, 1983. Currently, there are three volumes in print:
> *Building Your Own Theology: Volume 1, Introduction* (Second Edition). Boston: UUA, 2000.
> *Building Your Own Theology: Volume 2, Exploring* (Second Edition). Boston: UUA 2005.
> *Building Your Own Theology: Volume 3, Ethics*. Boston: UUA and Cleveland: United Board of Homeland Ministries, 1994.

Goldenberg, Samuel, Eleanor Hunting, and Mary Thomson. *In Our Hands, Grades 1-3: A Peace and Social Justice Program*. Boston: UUA, 1989.

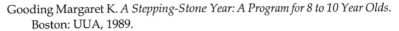

Gooding Margaret K. *A Stepping-Stone Year: A Program for 8 to 10 Year Olds.* Boston: UUA, 1989.

Gowdy, Nannene, Mary Ann Moore, and Marjorie Skwire. *Timeless Themes: Stories from the Hebrew and Christian Bibles for Grades 3 and 4.* Boston: UUA, 1991.

Hunting, Eleanor, Virginia Lane, and Harold Rosen. *In Our Hands: A Peace and Social Justice Program, Senior High.* Boston: UUA, 1990.

McDonald, Colleen M. *We Are Many, We Are One: A Unitarian Universalist Preschool Curriculum.* Boston: UUA, 1996.

Morrison-Reed, Mark. *How Open the Door: The Afro-American Experience in Unitarian Universalism.* Boston: UUA, 1989.

Meyer, Carol D. *Our Unitarian Universalist Story.* Boston: UUA, 1996.

Middleton, Betty Jo. *Special Times: Honoring Our Jewish and Christian Heritages for Grades 1 and 2.* Boston: UUA, 1994.

Navias, Eugene B. , ed., and Larry Philips, arr. *Bible Songs on Timeless Themes.* Boston: UUA, 1991.

Nelson, Roberta and Christopher. *Parents as Resident Theologians.* Boston: UUA, 1990.

------. *Parents as Social Justice Educators.* Boston: UUA, 1993.

------. *Parents as Spiritual Guides.* Boston: UUA, 2001.

Poinsett, Norma and Vivian Burns. *Rainbow Children: A Racial Justice and Diversity Program for Ages 5 to 8.* Boston: UUA, 1995.

Pratt, Debora Chandler. *Celebrating Me and My World: A Unitarian Universalist Preschool Curriculum.* Boston: UUA, 1995.

Ranck, Shirley. *Cakes for the Queen of Heaven.* Boston: UUA, 1986.

Reed, Christine and Patricia Hoertdoerfer. *Neighboring Faiths: Exploring Religion with Junior High Youth.* Boston: UUA, 1997.

Robertson, Frank, Margery Donn, Dorris Dow Alcott, Betty Jo Middleton, and Mary Ann Moore. *World Religions: A Year's Curriculum for Junior Youth.* David Marshak, ed., Boston: UUA, 1987.

Senn, Corelyn F. *Growing Times.* Boston: UUA, 1980.

Strong, Elizabeth May. *Messages in Music: Unitarian Universalism for Junior High.* Boston: UUA, 1993.

Washburn, Stephen C. *Conversations with the Bible: Spiritual Growth for Religious Liberals.* Boston: UUA, 1994.